A Complete Guide to Marketing Magazine Articles

A Complete Guide to Marketing Magazine Articles

Duane Newcomb

Cincinnati, Ohio

Library of Congress Cataloging in Publication Data

Newcomb, Duane G.
    A complete guide to marketing magazine articles.
    1970 ed. published under title: How to make big money free-lance writing.
    1. Authorship — Handbooks, manuals, etc.
I. Title.
PN161.N44   1975   808'.02   75-30827
0-911654-32-1

What This Book
Can Do for You

If you've always dreamed of writing for publication—wanted to add to your income—wanted to sell consistently—wanted to establish a successful writing career—or make really big money writing, this, then, is the book for you.

Learning to write and learning to make money writing—or even breaking into print—are two different things.

You can take all sorts of writing courses and read dozens of writing-technique books. Yet no matter how hard you study not one will bring you anywhere near making a living writing, let alone show you how to cash in on the really exciting rewards that free-lance writing offers.

Every writer who wants this has to stumble along finding his own way through trial and error. As a consequence, although there are millions of would-be writers in the United

States today and hundreds of thousands of publishing writers, you can count on both hands the ones making a reasonable income.

This, of course, is ridiculous.

Anyone who can write a clear sentence can easily learn to sell consistently.

This book doesn't fool around with writing platitudes. It explodes the technique myth and shows you step by step first the essential "marketing side" of breaking into print, then the techniques you must master if you expect to be a writer. The first five chapters explore the basics, showing you how to lay the foundation for future writing success—by learning first how to aim, then step by step how to find ideas that earn checks—how to focus and how to do a superior research job—all essentials of even the most elementary writing success.

The second third of this book shows you how to really start aiming for money, whether your goal is to add a good second income or establish yourself in a writing career. It again shows you step by step exactly how to establish yourself with editors, and from then on exactly how to aim for the big markets, focusing on money-making writing areas, and also how to make sure you're getting the maximum efficiency from everything you do.

The final section adds the extras you need to actually cash in. Making money writing is not hard, but it's certainly elusive to most writers. This section shows you the techniques all but a handful of writers miss.

It shows you how to make what you're already doing multiply your writing effectiveness hundreds of times. It shows you explicitly how to use the interest of your writing, not the principal; exactly how to turn out writing in volume at top quality —how to build your name and make it carry you to better-paying and more assignments, how to work into the top markets and build a solid success as you go. And finally how to make additional dollars by reselling much of the material you've already written.

This book is not intended to be read once and put aside. It is in effect a handbook for making a writing success. It takes you from the point where you more or less know writing technique but can't sell, to a really good yearly income. It must be read over and over again. Over the next few years, you'll find yourself coming back time and time again to see exactly how to handle some fine point.

In addition, many examples, charts, illustrations, step-by-step analyses, and reference materials are included to help you throughout your writing career. This, in short, is a book that offers much more than you can obtain from one reading. Over the years you'll be referring back to find where to send for certain information, where to write for pictures, where to go for reference material, exactly what format to use for certain types of markets, and more.

This book, of course, departs radically from many of the accepted writing theories and will stir up considerable controversy among teachers, editors, and a few purist writers.

Nevertheless, whether you are a beginner or a professional trying to learn the secrets of "How to Make Money Writing," this book will take you where you want to go!

DUANE NEWCOMB

Contents

14

*A Complete Guide
to
Marketing Magazine
Articles*

CHAPTER 1

How to Start

There's money to be made out there in the writing field and you, if you can write a letter other people can understand, can cash in on it. The basic key is your imagination.

If you've already sold a few pieces or are a consistently selling writer, you're ready to start right now learning how to really make money. If not, you're going to have to learn the basics. Fortunately, there are dozens of books that teach fundamentals. In addition, I will give you a system in this chapter which, if followed to the letter, will enable you to start selling right now.

This book, however, is not fundamentally one on how to write but on how to sell your writing. Over the years, teaching thousands of students, I've discovered there's a vast difference between teaching someone to write and teaching him to sell

17

what he writes. In addition, there's an even greater distance from a few sales to a consistently good writing income.

The difference is approach, and fortunately you don't have to be the best writer in the world to put these principles to work for you.

The purpose of this book, of course, is to show you how to make money writing. To do this, we're going to concentrate on the type of writing which you can sell in quantity. This means articles and related nonfiction material first—and books as a supplement later.

This does not mean fiction because the market has dropped out of slick fiction, and about the only way left to make money here is through confessions and fiction books. These fields, however, aren't for everyone—articles are.

Today there are approximately 15,000 publications all buying from four to 30 or more articles a month from free-lancers. Many are screaming for material. All you have to do to cash in on this bonanza is to write in a fairly logical manner, on a subject they are looking for, in a way to please their readers.

In my writing classes, I've had many students whom I consider only fair writers, yet they sell time and time again.

The secret to making money from writing lies primarily in training yourself to cash in on what skill you do have.

For instance, one of my students who decided to be a full-time money-making writer discovered he liked the education field and was interested in what was happening there. He started out writing articles about dropouts, then did several pieces about controversial education personalities, finally he started doing in-depth pieces about every phase of students, schools, and education personnel.

Last I heard of him, he was flying around the country gathering material from major colleges for a number of articles and several books on student unrest.

Another writer specializing in the business field consistently manages to turn his knowledge into good money everywhere he goes. This particular writer, for instance, knows that business magazines buy articles on stores, and can easily make $300 to $400 by just walking through a shopping center doing articles on the business operations he finds there.

There's money to be made everywhere for every magazine, it's just a matter of using your imagination until you come up with ideas which magazines will buy in volume.

As you go along in this book, then, I will help you begin to apply your imagination in a creative way so you can turn practically everything you see into money.

Another point I want to make right here is that making money free-lance writing doesn't necessarily mean making $1000, $2000, or $4000 from each article.

You may find, of course, that you want to work for the major magazines for $2000 an article, but that certainly isn't necessary to make money free-lance writing.

There are a limited number of magazines paying over $500 per article. But there are literally thousands paying in the $50 to $500 range. And these are the ones in which you can easily put together a good income.

This book is concerned with making big money from the entire wide magazine field (all 15,000 of them), no matter what magazines pay individually.

Don't let the $70 and $100 checks fool you. In this business they come easily, and as we go along, I'll show you how, even if you never see a $1000 check, you can still make money free-lance writing.

What you must realize, however, is that learning to make money free-lance writing means more than learning to turn out a few articles. It means getting so efficient that your dollar per hour rate soars. It means learning to get your production into high gear—bringing your rate per article as high as you can possibly get it—creating a demand for yourself as an article writer, and making your writing pay off many ways.

Today hundreds of thousands try to write, thousands sell, but only a handful make much money. Why? Because the others just haven't been able to master the techniques.

Fortunately, however, they're not terribly hard to develop. It just takes work.

In this book, I will show you all the necessary steps for profitable writing. But remember, these steps are far different from just learning to write, and you must master them all if you too intend to join the ranks of the professional writer.

START LAYING THE GROUNDWORK NOW

As I'm sure you can see here, the first step in selling consistently is to know who will buy what and to have plenty of backup material so you can come up with good, meaty articles that will really please the editors. Because of this, no matter what kind of a writer you are—beginner or expert—start laying the groundwork for even bigger and better sales right now. First, take a look at your files. Are you regularly accumulating material along the lines you're interested in—if not, get started. You're going to need it later.

Practically everywhere you turn in writing you are going to need some background and that's where your files come in.

One well-known writer, doing a piece on recreational vehicles, had all he needed about the vehicles and their use but needed some additional material showing sales volume and the number of people using the vehicles annually. Fortunately, some time ago he had started clipping everything he could find out of newspapers and magazines. Confronted with this problem, he simply went to his files, pulled out the material, inserted it in the proper place, and sent the article off. Simple? Sure it is —if you've got something to work from.

In the beginning, set up your files alphabetically—clip the items you're interested in and file. Many writers have very elaborate systems which they use; you may want to start out this way but you certainly don't have to.

The second thing you must start right now in laying the groundwork for future big money is magazine study. First, of course, you must have the magazines to look at. Since there are some 15,000 and maybe we can find only 200-300 on the newsstands, there's a problem. Most go to subscribers only. This means it's up to us to send for them.

Take out a copy of *Writer's Market,* turn to the category you're interested in, and write to the editors of the first five magazines, requesting a sample copy. (See Figure 1.)

Please send me a sample copy of your magazine plus a guide to writers, if available.

Thank you.

Name

Address

Figure 1. Postcard Form.

You should continue this throughout your writing career until you've built a substantial writing library to work from.

Since you must know which magazines are taking what and how they want it presented, you're going to have to look over all your possible markets.

You also should begin right now to study the magazines thoroughly. At this point, I suggest that you simply look over the articles they are taking and ask yourself, "Do I know anything or have I been doing anything in my field they might be interested in?" A good idea is to spend one hour every day looking over the magazines coming in, with an idea as to what they will take. There are more elaborate ways to study magazines, of course, which will let you zero in more closely, but we will get to this in a later chapter—right now it's enough that you get started.

Third, you must pick up basic techniques. Since this is a book on how to make money writing, many of you will have sold a number of pieces already. But you just haven't learned the techniques and attitudes necessary to parlay your sales into big money. For those of you who have yet to make your first sale, we'll give you a method right here for picking up fundamentals that we've found works wonders. This is simply the "learn by doing" technique. In my writing classes I've learned it isn't necessary to spend long hours on teaching basics. We simply do it, and correct our technique as we go along.

There are, however, some procedures that are essential. First we've got to remember that a "sold article" isn't just a piece of good writing. It consists of two parts, the writing itself and the magazine's requirements. This simply means that a good, solid piece of writing may well be turned down simply because it isn't handled in the manner the magazine wants it to be, it doesn't meet the needs of the readers, and for several other reasons.

Therefore, we must start out thinking not primarily in terms of learning to write but learning to satisfy the requirements of a magazine and its readers. For this reason I've devised a number of steps, which if followed carefully, result in sales many many times. Here they are:

1. Find the idea.

2. Look up possible markets using the system in Chapter 3.

3. Query the editor asking if he's interested.

4. Hope for a letter back saying "Yes, go ahead."

5. Look over the magazine and try to determine what approach works best for the reader—and how similar pieces are put together in the magazine—i.e.: if there are lots of statis-

tics, quotes from authorities, examples. Is it first, second, third person, etc.?

6. Organize the article.

7. Write it.

8. Revise it.

9. Check it, making sure it reads like the others in the magazine and it satisfies their readers' needs.

The entire secret here is not in just writing an article, but writing an article so it satisfies the needs and requirements of one particular magazine. The query is used to make you focus down and write it for that editor.

There are, of course, a number of facets to each of the above points. If you're at all weak here, I suggest you combine your use of this book with either *Writing the Modern Magazine Article* by Max Gunther, *The Writer Inc.*, or *Writing and Selling Non-Fiction*, by Hayes B. Jacobs, *Writer's Digest*.

DECIDE WHAT YOU WANT WHAT MAGAZINES, WHAT FIELDS, HOW MUCH MONEY

I don't mean do this right in the beginning, but start zeroing in within the first six months or so. Do you like the general magazines? Maybe your interest lies in the religious field and you should begin to think in that direction. Maybe you like juveniles—if you do, start thinking in that direction right now. In each field, of course, there will be some magazines you would like to hit more than others. In the general field, for instance, maybe you'd like to write for *Redbook, Holiday,* and some of the others. Of course, don't expect to hit your first choices immediately, but certainly begin to think in that direction—also begin to think of what kind of money you'd like to make.

What you will find is that you will change your desires and your sights as you go along—but know, for instance, that you want to make $20,000 a year out of your writing—then begin working toward that. I find it's best to set intermediate goals in the beginning, like, for instance, $200 a month or less, then raise it to $400, then to $800, and so on. You can usually move easily from say $600 a month to $700, but if you try to jump from $6000 a year to $40,000, the gap is almost impossible. However, if you say, "I'm just starting; I haven't made any sales yet, but I'm going to make $1000 or $2000 this year, then I'm going to work it up until eventually I'm making $25,000 a year"—that's possible, you have something we can work with and which will build as you go along.

And remember we're going to build our big-money income with all sizes of checks . . . . $20, $75, $200, $1000—and everything in between. Don't be fooled just because the individual check is small—they all add up.

START WITH ANY MARKET—
THEN KEEP PUSHING

It is kind of an old axiom that if you have a goal which you focus on, it doesn't really matter where you start. This is quite true of writing. If you're going to write for the largest magazines, you can easily start with the smallest and work your way up. And the minor markets are far easier to begin with. I tell my class and correspondence students in the beginning to concentrate on these magazines: 1. Young people's (juveniles); 2. Religious; 3. Newspaper features; 4. Business and trade publications; 5. Home and family; 6. Specialized publications such as camping, trailer, farm, retirement, and so forth.

These are magazines which don't get 10,000 or 20,000 manuscripts a year and are willing to work with a beginning writer.

For instance, Peter Dickinson, former editor of *Retirement Living* magazine, worked through four rewrites with one of my students to come up with a manuscript he considered suitable.

Each time Pete would come back with criticism—on the third try, he finally put a little note in which said, "If we don't hit it next time, let's quit"—but, being persistent, this student revised it the way the editor wanted it and sold the fourth time out.

Few of the larger markets will work with you that way—so the place to start if you haven't sold much is the smaller magazines where they are extremely receptive.

Unfortunately, at this point, I find many writers make a few sales and simply quit. One whose ambition was to sell *Sunset Magazine* worked and worked and worked with the manuscript until it was just right, sent it in, and sold it the first time out. This writer quit writing and hasn't done a piece since.

After you begin to sell, then you must start pushing and keep reaching out. Keep expanding your ideas and keep reaching for bigger and bigger money. The only way you'll ever make money free-lance writing is to continually be dissatisfied with what you're doing and the amount of money you're now making. There's great money to be made in this business. But you must go after it because you can easily get stuck along the way.

I can show you many writers who've been at this 15 or 20 years who now make $15,000 a year—but will never do any better—simply because they're satisfied and aren't willing to push on to new plateaus. They're stuck now and will never go any higher, not because they can't but because they've quit pushing.

TWO WAYS TO GO—VOLUME MARKETS
OR HIGH-PAYING ONES

You will have to decide somewhere along the line exactly how you're going to make your money writing. There are markets that will pay you $500, $1000, $2000, or $4000 for each individual sale. This way, of course, you can build volume with fewer units.

The only problem is that this type of article takes a great deal of time. I've done some in the $2000 range, for instance, that took 20 to 30 interviews, 30 to 40 phone calls, and many, many hours of research.

There's also another way to go. One $1000 check equals $1000 and so do ten $100 ones. The smaller checks also are a lot easier to come by. In my own case, I found after hitting the larger magazines a few times that this kind of writing didn't suit my temperament. I like to do one interview, one article. I found that, while I could do the more elaborately researched pieces, I did better financially if I concentrated on a lot of smaller checks. In the end, I turned out to be a production expert. I found I could easily produce 30 to 40 $100 articles a month without much trouble—whereas I had a hard time juggling all the elements required to do enough $1000 articles in a year to make a really good income.

There are two ways to do it then and it's going to depend on your temperament. You can put enough $25, $50, $100, and $200 articles together each year to make yourself an income in the $10,000 or up range or you can concentrate on less articles at a higher rate per article.

If you go in for the larger money per piece, you'll have to remember that there are a lot of details to attend to for each article you turn out. If you go for volume, you'll also have to remember that you're on a treadmill that goes faster and faster. There are all sorts of problems to solve. You must interview, take pictures, rewrite your manuscripts, juggle everything together, and still turn out 30 or 40 pieces a month.

After you've handled a few articles, however, you'll begin to see which way you want to head.

Actually the way today's market is going, I feel it's no longer wise to consider these methods as completely separate.

Recently several fairly high-paying markets have disappeared and more are sure to go. The magazine business really is bigger and better than ever—but it's different. The trend is to more specialized audiences for specific knowledge such as trailers, boats, skin diving, surfing, and more. These are the areas that are prospering.

The best way, then, seems to be to treat the whole field as one—a production market in which you may turn out a $50 article, then a $700 one . . . . and you spin off the $700 one into another $50 or $60 sale, and the $50 one into a $700 sale.

In addition, of course, books are a definite part of your program. In making big money, you will probably spin them off as you go about writing articles.

The reason for this is that for most people it takes a lot of article experience before they feel ready to write books, and by far the easiest and quickest way to build a good income is to employ all the money writing techniques available in the magazine field.

In this book, then, I shall show you how to use magazines to multiply your income and also how to add to it with additional book sales.

Checking on Chapter 1

Aiming for big money means learning to use a method. Constantly use your imagination to dig out ideas that add to your income.

You should start laying the groundwork. Build your subject-matter files in areas that interest you, by collecting and studying as many magazines as possible and by aiming your writing at magazine needs.

A. A "sold article" consists of two things, good writing and a magazine's requirements—you must have both to sell consistently.

B. You can learn to write easily by drafting a piece directly for a particular magazine.

Decide what areas and magazines you'd like to work for. Then, as quickly as possible, start working in that direction.

Start with any market you like. You should begin small and keep pushing until you get where you want to go.

Big money can be made two ways: By selling a few articles to large magazines for big checks or by learning to turn out many articles for smaller checks.

CHAPTER 2

How to Put the Odds
in Your Favor

In this book I'm going to show you how to make a career of free-lance writing. Know right now that you can do it!

Not overnight maybe, but if you'll start now, follow the rules laid down here, and stay with it, you can make it.

Making good money, of course, means mastering a number of disciplines—the first of which is learning how to tilt the odds in your favor so the manuscript you send in really hits the spot and lets the editor know you understand his publication and his problems, and are the one writer who can help solve them.

Each year, of course, hundreds of thousands send manuscripts to magazines. The majority of these are sent right back with a rejection slip. *Redbook* alone gets over 70,000 pieces of mail a year from writers, and buys about four articles a year that aren't either assigned or solicited in some way. Even

Retirement Living, a magazine in the retirement field, gets 300 manuscripts a month out of which they may take about 15—if we look at all the manuscripts going to the big magazines, then, we may say that our chances of selling to one of them could be 10,000 to 1—and to the smaller magazines—possibly 100 to 1.

But hold on there! In class we prove this is wrong every day. I've had students sell to *Redbook* on their second or third article, and also we sell dozens of other articles to all types of magazines.

First, we have to realize that the odds are not quite what they seem. There are approximately 15,000 magazines in the United States taking free-lance material and the big magazines are the ones that receive the majority of manuscripts. You may find the smaller ones, especially the trade journals, get only a few more each year than they can use.

In the second place, you must realize the way writers are. Most writers want to write what they want to write—not what the magazine readers want to read. And they automatically cut themselves out of a market.

What happens, I've found, is that writers just pick out a topic and write an article. However, as we've discussed before, writing is only about half of getting an article in print. After all, magazine editors try to please their readers and have individual ways of putting articles together. In addition, of course, some magazines try to give the impression they're staff written, which means all articles must read alike.

You'll find that the majority of articles in some magazines are in the first person . . . . some don't allow dialogue . . . . others like a lot of examples . . . . still others put everything in the direct address. All of this a writer must take into consideration when he's trying to make his writing pay off big.

This one factor alone probably accounts for 90 per cent of all rejections. *Parade* magazine still gets fiction, and I don't think they've ever taken any. Writers somehow forget that magazines are a limited market, which take only certain categories done in certain ways to interest their readers; because they don't sit down, study the readership, and send the magazines exactly what they want, most writers fail. You, however, can be an exception. And you should never pay any attention to the odds. The secret is to analyze the market and give that market exactly what it wants. If you do this thoroughly, you can cut the odds from say, 1000 to 1 to almost 50-50—or maybe in the beginning 80-20. But that's still pretty good considering the hundreds of thousands of other writers that are trying.

MAGAZINES BUY IDEAS THAT SATISFY READERS

We must realize magazines are a business. They exist because people buy magazines and patronize advertisers whose ads appear in their pages. Readers read these magazines because they're supplying some information they can use or need. Primarily people read magazines today to get information they can use in their own lives. A woman, for instance, may pick up a woman's magazine to look for decorating tips, or different ways to fix her hair, or she may want to read about something that's affecting her child or family. In this type of magazine she probably wouldn't want to read about a new car test because that's beyond her interest range.

The same is true of other magazines—they specialize in readers interested in certain types of things and get their readership because they confine their articles to those subjects.

Let's take an example: *Guns Magazine* is likely to feature articles such as: "Test Report on Inexpensive .45 Kit"; "H & R .17 Wildcat"—"Field Test of a First Commercial .17 Rifle"; "Saga of the Colt Six Shooter"—"Excerpt from a Brand New Book, *Firearms Archeology*"; "What Should a Rifle Weigh?"— "Rifle Head Is Important to Good Shooting"; "Turkey Shoot"— "Tips on Having Fun with a Scatter Gun"; "The New S. I. G. A & P Rifle"—"Newest Import in the Military/Sporter Field";

"Guns at the NRA Show—A Visit to Each of the Exhibits"; "Experts Choice"—"Color Feature–Colt Single Action"; "Reflections of a Gun Hunt"; "Free Gun Drawing"; "Factors for One-Shot Kills"—"Two Considerations for Better Game Harvest."

Now this is a good example of a magazine's single-mindedness. All articles are aimed at the gun buff. There's a wide range from tests, turkey shoots, and how to kill game, but they still all revolve around one single theme—guns.

Obviously an article on how to raise a baby would be silly here. This is awfully basic, yet writers still do these things.

Now let's look at *Family Circle*. A recent issue lists: "The Marriage Poll"; "Who Is Smarter–Husband or Wife?"; "Inside 'Dear Abby' "; "From Our Outdoor Cook–Best of the Cookbooks"; "On the Same Simple Unpainted Chest–Five Absolutely Beautiful Finishes"; "Set Yourself a Layered Look Wardrobe That Really Takes Off"; "How to Talk to Your Teen"; "How to Look Great in Glasses"; and "Williamsburg Samplers to Stitch." This, then, is a woman's magazine—articles revolve around marriage and family, food, crafts, fashions, childcare, beauty, and similar homemaking items and skills. Everything basically is oriented this way. To put the odds in your favor, you must offer something in a similar vein.

The real secret of putting the big-money odds in your favor is to analyze the magazines thoroughly until you know them backwards and forwards—until you know what topics they take, until you know what their readers like, and literally until you can predict what's going to be in the magazine as well or better than the editor. Once you can do this, you will begin "hitting" that magazine regularly, and the editor will feel you understand thoroughly what he's trying to do.

The way we do it in class, basically, is to pick up a magazine and read these areas thoroughly: (1) the editorials; (2) the columns; (3) Letters to the Editor; (4) the ads; (5) the articles themselves, especially their titles.

(1) *The Editorials:* This will, more or less, give you some idea of how an editor looks at life and what he thinks his readers want. The secret here is to decide who the reader is, and basically what he wants to read. To do this, we have to analyze. For instance, if you look at *Cosmopolitan,* Helen Gurley Brown's "Step into My Parlor" is where she talks to readers. In a recent issue she points out exactly how Managing Editor, George Walsh, makes up a schedule several months in advance by selecting one emotional article, a health subject, a career story, a first person reminiscence, a serious piece about industry or the world situation, one or two profiles, and a quiz—along with 16 regular columns and departments such as beauty, fashion, travel, and food. This type of material, of course, gives you a wealth of information on what a magazine like *Cosmopolitan* actually takes.

(2) *The Columns:* Here, again, is where we begin to see the magazines' ideas of what their readers want to read. If we look in *Cosmopolitan* again, we find these columns: "*Cosmo* Reads a New Book"; "*Cosmo* Listens to Records"; "*Cosmo* Goes to the Movies"; "*Cosmo's* 10-Minute Gourmet Dinner": "June Horoscope"; "Your Love Horoscope"; "Analyst's Couch"; "The Travel Bug"; "Dieter's Notebook"; "Hip Housekeeping"; "Speak Easy–The Art of Speaking Clearly"; "*Cosmo* Tells All"; "*Cosmo* Shopper"; "Directory of Schools and Colleges"; and "Dear *Cosmo*" (letters).

Now just looking at these columns begins to tell you what kind of readers this magazine attracts and how they look at life. The fact that *Cosmo* runs "Your Love Horoscope" means it primarily caters to women readers—but when you realize it also includes a column called "Analyst's Couch"—this means its readers are probably of above average intelligence and are concerned about the more sophisticated things in life. "Hip Housekeeping" and similar items, however, indicate they also are concerned with everyday problems.

Now look at what the columns themselves say. *Here we begin to get the idea that basically this reader is a single woman*

—or one with those ideas—who wants to get the most out of life and is interested in men or is quite man oriented.

(3) **Letters to the Editor:** What better place to find out about readers' interests than from the readers themselves. Be sure to read this section when you're trying to get an idea of what a magazine is all about.

In a recent issue of *Cosmo*, for instance, one of the letters to the editor describes in complete detail what the reader liked about the article ("Lilly Bart's Pleasure of a Temporary Affair"). She then went into detail describing her own life, her reaction to the article, and other points, giving you a good insight into the reader herself and what she wants to read about.

(4) **The Ads:** This is probably the most important reading you'll ever do. The reason is that advertisers advertise the items in the magazine they think readers will buy. By looking at them, you can begin to get an idea of the reader himself, his income, his religion, what he will think about contemporary issues, and more.

For instance, if you pick up a magazine and it says "How Would You Like to Get Your High School Diploma at Home?" –or "Send for This Pamphlet on Your Career as a Diesel Mechanic"–or you see an advertisement that says "Body Building Made Easy"—you'll assume this is a middle-low income reader, with not too much education, and one who works on a blue collar job.

On the other hand, suppose they're advertising Lincoln Continentals, yachts, smart clothes, and high-price golf bags. You then know that this is a man who's probably quite social, has a better than average income, and is interested in a great many leisure activities.

By looking at the ads, noting the types of items, their price, and more or less the cultural direction, you can begin to figure out the reader's inner self.

After you've studied the ads carefully, see if you can answer these questions: (1) Is this reader a man or woman? (2) How much education does he have? (3) What's the average income? (4) What's the religion? (5) What does he think about the three leading issues in the news today? (6) What are his major interests and hobbies?

If you can do this successfully, you can begin to design articles that will interest this reader and consequently put the odds in your favor.

(5) *The Articles Themselves:* In this case, look at the titles and the subtitles and simply try to feel the article direction. I believe these are the least important of all in forming your image of who the reader is. Probably the most valuable are the ads and the letters to the editor. But by all means read the titles through and try to get an idea of things the magazine thinks their readers would like to read about.

HOW TO MAKE SURE YOUR IDEA HITS THE BIG-MONEY BULL'S-EYE

This will be difficult in the beginning, but you'll get better as you go along. After you've tried this for awhile, you'll know when you get an idea whether the magazine you're interested in will take it or not and exactly which magazine will be interested.

The way to do it is simply this: first of all, take your idea and try to match it to the magazine (in a later chapter, we'll show you exactly how to find markets that will be interested in your idea). Take that magazine and determine exactly who your reader is. Then, determine the categories of articles that the magazine buys. Ask yourself "Will this reader be interested in my idea? Does it fit one of the categories the magazine is taking? Finally, is it the angle the magazine is taking to please their readers?" Take some magazines and go back through and look at the angles they're taking within your category.

LOOK OVER THE MAGAZINE YOU WANT TO HIT AND TRY TO FIND ARTICLES THAT FIT YOUR EXPERIENCE

The only way you can match your ideas to the magazine is to read and find out what they're doing. To do this, you will need to read several issues because some of the seasonal topics appear only once a year. *Field and Stream,* for instance, regularly has features on camping and boating in the early part of each year—but not in every issue.

It's best if you try to categorize articles by topics. Then, as you read article titles and subtitles, try to remember happenings from your own experience or things that you've heard about that will fit a topic category—this will make it possible to offer the magazine ideas you're familiar with and want to do—that all tie into the magazine's *needs.*

Here's how to do it—let's look at *Field and Stream.* In a recent issue, you'll see a title that says "New Way for Surf Stripers." The subtitle says "With a kite stabilizing your bait in the surf, you stay warm and dry on the beach while you fish for stripers in the coastal waters of the mid-Atlantic. This is fishing for stripers with a kite."

Maybe you have developed or have seen an interesting and new way of fishing. Let's say you have run into somebody some time ago who uses a small rocket to shoot their bait way out in the water. You should be triggered by this and realize that this is a similar category to what's appearing here.

The next article says, "About Mushrooms–Where Anglers Go, Mushrooms Grow." This is an article on mushrooms— which ones are edible, which are not. Now since they've done something on mushrooms, they probably wouldn't be interested in anything more along that line, but there are other things in this category. For instance, maybe edible plants that fishermen can use that would also be an outdoor delicacy—possibly you have done something on this and could suggest an article—or plants that can save a hunter's life—and more.

The next article is, "Who Says Propellers Are Obsolete?" These are noisemaking surface plugs—if you're a fisherman, maybe you'll have something along this line. If not, pass it by.

The next one is "Jigging for Bass–East Tennessee Style." This is a regional twist on a way to fish—again, if you've got something unusual along this line, fine; if not, pass it by.

The next article says, "Paradise for *Plunker*," a how-to on fishing for steelhead on the Columbia—they use a bell to let them know when the fish are on—again, this is unusual, but if you have something that's novel like this, you might want to try it.

The next article is, "Pork Rind and Bluegill." This is a how-to article for fishermen, how to use pork rind with all sorts of lures. Again, how-to articles always have more of a reception than fishing-type articles. And if you have a way of doing something, then you'll want to give it a try. Maybe you have a different way of baiting a hook, or tieing flies, or scouting a stream, or a 1001 other how-to's—all are good.

The next article is, "Turtle Clapping"—how to snag turtles.

The next, "Float for First-Class Fishing." This is an article on float fishing in Montana. If you have made a trip with a little different angle, you might want to give it a try.

Another one says, "Horse Sense." What a sportsman should know about horses—packing, riding, etc. This should trigger a number of "how-to's" in the mountains—maybe how to establish a base camp, maybe the ABC's of Jeep travel in the backcountry—how to construct a lean-to, and other skills that are basic.

The main thing here is to look at the article, try to categorize what they're doing, such as an unusual fishing trip, basic how-to, where to go, etc., and try to see if there's something in your experience that's similar to this.

THE QUICKEST ROUTE TO SALES
IS THROUGH TOPICS AND MAGAZINES
YOU FEEL MOST AT HOME WITH

You'll find in writing magazine articles that it's best to restrict yourself to the ideas, material, and magazines you like and feel comfortable with. For instance, maybe you are a fisherman and like doing articles on fishing, but you have no feel at all for cooking. Therefore, you do articles on fishing and avoid those on cooking. This is a silly example, but many beginning writers stab out in all directions trying to do all sorts of articles —and, in many cases, for fields which they don't even like.

The same is true of magazines. Take a look at 15 or 20 magazines on the stands and ask yourself how you feel about them. For instance, go through a copy of *Woman's Day.* Do you like the articles? Do you like the way the magazine presents them? Do you feel comfortable with the material? If you do, then, you might want to try some articles for *Woman's Day.* But suppose you pick up *Pageant* and just don't seem to like the way the magazine is handled. Even if you'd like to see an article of yours in *Pageant* now, I'd advise you not to.

Now let me give you an example from my own experience. I've been writing for *Trailer Life Magazine* for years. I like the way the magazine feels, I like the way the articles are presented, I like everything about it. As a consequence, I have a real feel for this magazine and I can do articles that are similar to what they're already doing which have good reader appeal.

On the other hand, *Westways* magazine (a magazine of the Automobile Club of Southern California) has articles which are similar. For instance, looking at an issue of *Trailer Life,* you'll find titles such as "The Indians Are Waiting–Take Your Trailer to a Reservation," "Pickup Gold," "Be a Weekend Prospector," there's one on Hawaii, "Land of Sweet Leilani." Now looking at *Westways,* we see an article on "Surveying the Ski Scene," "Let's Explore a Byway," "Picnicking in the San Gabriels," "A Day in the City," "Christmas on Olivera Street," and more. Actually, while they both publish articles which are quite different, they also publish some which have a similar theme. However, I wouldn't any more try to get in *Westways* than I would fly. I just can't seem to get the angle they're using. What I'm really saying is that I just don't like the way they approach their articles. If you pin me down, I can't tell you exactly what it is—I just know I don't like it and I know I don't want to write that way. If I tried, I'd undoubtedly fail. As you go along you'll have to decide for yourself which magazines affect you this way—but believe me, some will.

CHECK AND RECHECK YOUR FINAL ARTICLE
WITH THE MAGAZINE IN MIND

When you finish your article and it sounds pretty good to you, you should then go back over it, keeping in mind your reader, and the way the magazine presents its material to the reader. Then try to decide if you are meeting these requirements. Later on I'll give you a checklist which will take apart the inner workings of your article, but here's one that will help you obtain a magazine's slant in a general way and help considerably in tilting the odds in your favor.

(1) Taking into consideration the titles used in the magazine I want to hit, is this the best possible title for my article? Does it create interest?

(2) Is this article the right length for this magazine? Or is it too long or too short? Are my facts true? If not, get on the phone and make sure.

(3) Is this article right for the market I'm going to send it to? Read two or three other articles in the magazine, then read yours again and see if it has the same "ring."

(4) Is this article presentable? Make sure it looks good before you send it out. Please don't send out a messy manuscript. If you've made more than one correction per page, type that page over.

Checking on Chapter 2

Don't pay any attention to writing odds. Most writers fail because they don't tailor their articles directly to the magazines and their readers. You can overcome this.

Magazines buy ideas that satisfy their readers. Most magazines cater directly to their readers' needs. You can determine what the editor thinks his readers want by looking at the articles he's now offering. All you have to do then is offer a different aspect of the themes the magazine is already using.

You must analyze magazines to do a good job. Do this by reading the editorials, departments, special features, ads, articles and titles, and picture captions. Try to form a mental image of the reader in your mind . . . . and offer ideas and writing of interest to that reader.

Try to match what you know with the magazine's needs. The easiest way to do this is to go through a magazine article by article, and try to come up with something out of your background or something you're familiar with that's in the same category as that particular article . . . . and is just as good. These are the article ideas you want to offer.

The key to selling is doing what you like. It's a lot easier to hit magazines you like with topics you enjoy than it is to force yourself. Usually the first time you look at a magazine, you can tell if you enjoy its style. These are the magazines you should aim at first.

You can put the odds in your favor by making sure your slant is right for the magazine you're sending a manuscript to. Do it by checking the titles with the ones the magazine's using, the article length, the market feel, and its appearance. These four things help tip odds in your favor and start you on the path toward constant sales.

CHAPTER 3

Where to Get Ideas

Just where do article ideas come from? Actually the inexperienced writer marvels at the variety of subjects a professional writer finds to write about. I and most of the professionals I know can sit at our desks and think up enough article ideas in an hour to last for the next three months. In addition, everywhere we go article ideas keep popping up.

Recently I did a houseboat test article for *Family Houseboating* magazine and found myself faced with several ideas before I left the dock.

In the first place, the boat itself was going to be used as a floating biology laboratory in a different type of new school for teen-agers (probably several articles here, including a story on the school's founder); second, the owner of the yacht sales who had just sold this particular boat had a very unique method of doing business (probably a trade journal piece); finally, about the middle of the afternoon, a public relations firm brought in two teen-age models and took pictures for a school brochure (this probably could have been worked around one way for a teen magazine, another for a trade journal). Since I had my hands full doing the houseboat test article itself, I simply let everything else go and just did the one article. Actually, however, I find that for every article I do I probably reject ten to 15 other good ideas.

As you begin to recognize just what magazines are looking for, you too will see article possibilities everywhere. You must, of course, develop a nose for news (that is the ability to sense what people want to read about). As you go along, however, you will train yourself to look at every person, every experience, and every event with the idea that here is a possible article some reader will be interested in.

Now let's define what an article idea is. In short, it is merely some subject, such as education, and some angle, that a group of readers might be interested in hearing about.

To show you how this works let's take the subject of education. Now that's not an article idea, but a subject—to make it an acceptable magazine idea, you must put an angle on it. To do this simply start asking yourself questions.

Are we spending too much money on education today? Should we pay our teachers more? Just what should we do with the faster-learning student? Is education today anticreative? Are we giving our children the wrong values? Does education need to get back to basics?

You can go on and on with this list. Every angle here is a possible article idea that some group of readers probably will want to read about. No matter how many questions you ask, you'll find somebody would like to know the answer. (You can also, of course, put these angles in the form of statements instead of questions—but questions seem the easiest.)

This actually is all there is to finding an article idea— there are a lot of other ins and outs, of course, but you will pick these up as you go along.

Now let's look at some other subjects and see what we can do.

Possible Article Ideas

Subjects	*Angle*
Trees	1. Can trees add more liveability to your yard?
	2. Are you using trees creatively in your landscaping?
	3. What makes trees drop their leaves?
	4. Just how does a tree grow?
Restaurants	1. Is restaurant service getting worse?
	2. Can specialty restaurants increase your living enjoyment?
	3. Can you use these famous restaurant recipes in your own cooking repertoire?
Camping	1. Which camping trailer for you?
	2. Can you camp with children and like it?
	3. Just how do you start camping?
	4. What equipment do you need?
	5. Do women belong in the campground?
	6. Are you a camping widow?
Telephone Books	1. Do you know how much information there is in a telephone book?
	2. Does a telephone book give you instant everything?
	3. What does it take to put out a telephone book?
Cars	1. How does your car compare with others?
	2. Are your reaction times good enough?
	3. Can you get more gas mileage?
	4. Is your car really safe?

While this may be a little oversimplified, it's all there is to it. Simply look at every situation you run into and start asking questions. Some of them, of course, will be better than others—but this is because some groups of readers (and therefore magazines) are more interested in some angles than others.

The trick is to match the subject and angle with the magazine's interest.

Now one other thing: There are some subjects which have been treated so often that the common angle is no longer of real interest. This doesn't mean there is no article idea here, it simply means you will have to add another angle—an angle on an angle.

Let's go back to our subject, education. An angle here might be, *can we do something about dropouts.* You will recognize this as a subject and an angle that has been gone over in magazines time and time again. It has peaked, gone down, and is no longer of real interest. But if we can add another good angle to it, an angle that some group of readers will still be interested in, then we have an idea that's salable *now.*

So what is it? Well, let's ask a question, can we take a dropout and turn him into a super-student? This might take the form of a professor who feels that dropouts make the best super-student prospects, or a school that's doing wonders with dropouts in a brand new way, or a study that shows people who have been out six months are all fired up to learn and can learn faster than others.

Of course, probably none of these can come directly off the top of your head. You'll have to do extra research, and find situations, such as the school, which are just right. But it can be done. So to make a stale idea salable, all you have to do is add another timely angle.

One additional consideration here in finding article ideas is to try to pick out those that are of vital importance to readers.

Hayes B. Jacobs in his book, *A Complete Guide to Writing and Selling Non-Fiction,*[1] points out that some of the basic human drives are sexual gratification, maternal behavior, hunger-thirst, aggressiveness, self-preservation, flight from danger, self-

---

[1] Hayes B. Jacobs, *A Complete Guide to Writing and Selling Non-Fiction* (Writer's Digest, 1967).

assertiveness, gregariousness, acquisitiveness, filial, paternal, and prematernal feelings and motives . . . . and good vital articles should be concerned with these basic drives.

Articles on home ownership, insurance, spare-time earning projects, collections, beauty care, and similar pieces, for instance, satisfy the basic drive for acquisitiveness.

Articles on food preparation, dieting, weight control, wine lore, and similar pieces satisfy the hunger and thirst drives.

Articles on what to do in case of fire, why you should stop smoking, how to survive earthquakes . . . . all have to do with the drive for self-preservation.

If you keep these drives in mind when selecting ideas, you'll readily see that some are of vital concern to the reader, some less so. Since there are many, many ideas, you should try to select those that people are really concerned with right now.

For instance, an article by Murray Teigh Bloom in the *Reader's Digest* called "They Brought Home the Wrong Baby" caused an enormous uproar all over the Midwest—was run across eight columns at the top of one page by the *Detroit Free Press* and caused many hospitals to tighten up their baby identification system. Why? Because the subject vitally affected people everywhere.

JUST WHAT IDEAS MAKE MONEY?

Practically every article idea will make money. It just depends on finding the right audience (and the right magazine). But somebody will buy every idea you can think up.

Now stop right here and realize that the whole purpose of this book is to show you how to sell what you write. Some of you will be surprised that instead of talking about big checks all the time, I talk about all sorts of amounts for articles from $10 up. Making big money writing doesn't necessarily mean getting a large amount for each article, it means learning techniques which give you lots of checks and multiply the ones you do get so the total is large.

Since there are literally thousands of articles being bought each month, it means that anyone with persistence can learn to make money free-lance writing . . . . and it isn't necessary to compete with writers in the major markets to do it either. In fact in many cases, if you follow these techniques, you'll find your income is far greater than theirs. Of course, if you want to aim for the top markets, by all means include it in your program . . . . but don't put all your eggs in that basket—especially not in the beginning.

Now back to making money from an idea. Some ideas, of course, bring in more than others. Making more money from a single idea, however, usually means it meets one of two requirements.

It's an idea that a magazine thinks its readers will particularly like, or it is an idea that with a little bit of modification can be sold to many, many magazines.

For instance, consumerism has become extremely important recently in the business magazine field. As a result, I started doing interviews with customers in stores on various business problems. Since this was a different approach, I asked and got about 20 per cent more for the idea than I would for a regular business article.

This was fine but I decided if we took these same problems and did a roundup—asking customers how they felt about the problem, manufacturers how they felt about it, dealers how they felt about it, and added the government's point of view—we would have something of real value to the magazine and to its readers. As a result, I asked and got almost five times what I ordinarily received for the other articles and one magazine even wanted to do it in book form.

In another case, I asked the editor of *Retirement Living* magazine about doing a piece on mobile homes and trailer living. In this case it wasn't going to be a typical piece dealing with mobile homes or trailers but a complete roundup, including the requirements for getting started, how people like living in them, how to buy, what to look for, and many, many other details.

This was, in short, above and beyond the normal run of articles. As a result, I asked for and received *double* my usual rate of pay.

So, for an idea which offers greater detail, and something more than the normal for the reader, you can expect to get more money.

How do you tell? The answer is intensive study. Go through the last 12 issues of the magazine, decide what they are doing, decide what a good subject for them would be, then offer something really extra. When you begin to get the feel of it, this system can't fail.

IDEAS THAT CAN BE SOLD MANY WAYS

Another good way to get more money on your way to a big-money income, of course, is to pick an idea that can be used in many magazines—or to simply find all the possible magazines for your ideas.

A good example of this is a trip of mine through California's gold country several years ago. I reasoned that a lot of people would be interested in this area because of its importance to the historic, old gold rush days of 1849.

Now I had a good topic. But what could I do with it? I sat down and decided it would make a good straight travel article. Campers would be interested, trailerists would like it, and so would many others. Also there were a lot of side activities along the way I could turn into money.

Here's what I came up with: "How to Camp California's Gold Country" (*Camping Guide* magazine), "How to Trailer California's Gold Country" (*Trail-R-News**), "Pan for Gold in California's Gold Country" (*Trailer Life*), "Gold Strike Mobile Home Park" (*Trailer Topics**), "Skin Diving for Gold" (*Camper Coachman*), "Skin Diving for Gold" (*Ford Truck Times* and *Skin Diver* magazine) and finally, "Travel in California's Gold Country" to several newspapers. This, then, could be turned many ways.

---

*discontinued

Article ideas are everywhere. You can stand on any street corner and find hundreds. In the beginning, you won't be able to see them—but as you begin to think of what readers are particularly interested in, it will start to clear up.

Start asking yourself why? What's behind this? What are the reasons for this and, finally, who would be interested in reading about it?

A few years ago a student saw people going across the street into a park carrying picnic lunches. He wondered where the idea got started, what were some of the unusual picnics that have taken place, and just what's behind a picnic anyway. Finished and illustrated with some popular local picnic spots, it became an article for the local newspaper.

Another student passing a florist shop saw a row of seven credit card decals on the window. Immediately he asked himself why they were there, just what this florist got out of them, and why would a reader like to read about it.

He walked in, introduced himself, interviewed the owner, and found this was one of the man's best sales tools. In addition, other florists would be interested because it meant more money to them. The article brought a check from *Southern Florist* magazine.

Finally, a student having to put her husband on a special noncholesterol diet wondered if other people wouldn't be interested. Written up, this brought a $200 check from *Mature Years* magazine. Literally, everything you do or see can be turned into money.

Here then are some places to find money-making ideas:

1. *Conventions:* All sorts of material comes out of every convention. Everything a speaker says, or every booth, can be turned into money.

One young woman attending a secretarial convention came up with: (1) an article on how to be a better secretary, (2) ten tips to get more out of your secretary, and (3) a career piece for juveniles entitled, "So You'd Like to Be a Secretary."

2. *Professions and Businesses:* This is probably one of the most lucrative fields. People like to read about outstanding people in businesses and professions. And business and professional people like to read about how their own members are doing a better job.

In addition, the market is huge—besides the general consumer magazines, there are well over 2500 business magazines that buy articles.

To do a good job here, you'll have to interview the person involved, tell the readers exactly how he did what he did in detail, and illustrate it with good solid pictures.

Once you master the marketing techniques, however, and realize that practically every magazine is interested in these if the subject appeals to their readers, the rest is easy.

For instance, an article on a man who makes family coats of arms as a profession appeared in *Grit,* and the Sunday *Mercury-News* magazine section.

An article on an unusual builder appeared in *Reader's Digest,* an article on a man who made a fortune out of potatoes appeared in *Fortune,* an article on how a man converted his department to data-processing equipment and how it is used to keep up vehicles, appeared in *Grounds Maintenance* magazine. An article on how a local storeowner catered to the growing recreational horse business in his neighborhood, by selling saddles and feed, appeared in *Farm Supply.* The list goes on and on.

3. *Home and Gardens:* There's probably nothing more lucrative than your own home or garden. Ideas are everywhere. Magazines buy a tremendous number of articles on how to grow a better lawn, how to select the right plant, how to remodel your house, how to do a better decorating job, and much, much more.

In fact, there are at least 19 magazines devoted exclusively to homes, gardens, and workshop items. Besides this, many, many others, including the women's magazines, the men's magazines, and the popular science group take hundreds of articles every year devoted to nothing but this subject.

Gene Weise, a California writer, supplements his regular income in his spare time by writing up his own home projects. In the past he has sold short pieces to *Popular Mechanics* on a new type of saw guard he designed himself, how to install a night light in the hall using the bell transformer, how to make a funnel for home use from a Clorox bottle, and more.

In short, practically everything around the home will make money if presented in the right way.

4. *Outdoor Travel:* What a great bonanza this is for the free-lance writer. Just look around you and everything suddenly becomes salable.

What are the new trends? Houseboating, recreational vehicles, dune buggies, different kinds of motorcycles, skin diving, the whole scope of outdoor recreation.

Let's look at the magazines: Recent issues of *Argosy* include articles on "Spend Your Vacation in the Saddle," "The New Outboards," "Make Your Alaskan Vacation Pay for Itself by Gold Panning," and more. *Family Circle* recently featured an article on "The True Facts About Camping." *Popular Mechanics* ran pieces on "The Wildest Boat Trip in the World," "Make Your Next Camp-out by Boat," and more. *Popular Science* featured "Your Guide to Camping on Wheels," "Rules of the Road and Campsite Tips," and "How to Enjoy All the Comforts of Home on Wheels."

In short it's almost impossible to pick up a magazine today that doesn't carry articles about some outdoor activity. This, of course, means unusual opportunities for anyone interested in this field.

5. *Your Health:* What magazine today doesn't feature titles like "How to Exercise for Better Health," "Seven Ways to a Slimmer You," "A Heart Diet That Really Works," "Exercise Without Really Working," and others?

A whole magazine, *Fitness for Living,* is devoted exclusively to enjoying exercise.

If you like to hike, enjoy jogging, like to try new diets, or are interested in medicine and its related fields, you'll find the health area an excellent market.

6. *Crafts, Mechanics, and Hobbies:* Articles on how to do or how to make something are in great demand. A mechanic's or carpenter's workshop or your own home repairs will provide plenty of material. Simply start looking at every hobby, craft, or do-it-yourself project with the idea in mind that it can be turned into a money-making article. Here are some recent titles from *Popular Science, Science and Mechanics,* and *Family Circle:* "A Model Hydroplane Skims the Water," "Those Way Out Wall Coverings" (collecting different decorative wall coverings), "This $16 Kit Makes You a Whiz at Model Rocketry," "Add a Rest to Your Lathe," "Build This Airplane for $1200," "Tool Kit for the Weekend Mechanic," "Package It Smashing with Paper" (how to decorate packages), "What on Earth Is This Family Doing?" (spatter-dying plain sheets for color explosion), "Fabulous New Notions in Easter Eggs" (how to decorate Easter eggs creatively).

In addition, my students have sold articles on their husband's model railroad hobby, on a man who wears a suit of rare coins, one who has a fantastic gun collection, another who is building an airplane in his garage, one whose hobby is the weather, and practically everything else under the sun.

7. *Prominent or Interesting Persons:* When I say prominent, I don't mean celebrities, but everyday people doing something interesting. Let me show you what I mean.

One of my students discovered a retired school teacher who was taking helicopter lessons to help her get to her mine in San Diego (just a little different). Articles on her sold to the local newspaper magazine section, *Retirement Living* (a retirement magazine), *Grit* (the largest weekly newspaper in the United States), and more.

We also found a man who taught the neighborhood children seamanship every weekend. This sold quickly to the magazine section of the local newspaper.

A retiree who started an employment center for other retirees, sold to *Retirement Living,* was picked up by another national magazine, and brought hundreds of letters.

Finally a local man who specialized in moving houses—and everything else—sold to three national magazines and is still going strong.

It isn't necessary to look for celebrities—just people who are doing something interesting.

8. *Experience:* Please never downgrade your own experiences. Everything that happens to you and everything that will happen can (if you think about it long enough) be made into articles that will bring good money.

Simply decide what angle of your experiences someone else would be interested in reading about. Here are a few examples:

1. "Snake in My Sleeping Bag"—(a *Reader's Digest* first-person article). I hope you don't have this one.

2. "We Went Camping in a Canyon"—a story about a couple who camped with a camper in a canyon.

3. "How I Converted a Wrecked Airplane into a Trailer"—a *Trailer Life* sale.

4. "I Was a Male Den Mother"—a story about a man who wanted his son to be in cubs but couldn't find a woman to take the den. This one sold to *This Week.**

5. "How I Make Christmas Candles"—sold to *Sunset* magazine by a woman whose hobby is candles.

6. "My Daughter Is a Nature Lover"—sold to *Mother's Manual*—simply my own experiences with a daughter who is constantly bringing bugs, butterflies, birds, and other wild creatures into the house and how she and I reacted to them.

All of these are fairly simple ideas that make good articles. The trick obviously is to know who wants to buy a piece on your experiences. We'll get back to this further on.

9. *Family Problems:* This is similar to experience, but

---

*discontinued

WHERE TO GET IDEAS

every family problem from child raising, to marriage to divorce, to taking care of older parents is something everyone is interested in. If you have a solution or an observation, then somebody wants to read about it. Simply consider the problems you and your family have and how you've managed to solve them.

For instance, my students have sold many articles on getting your child ready for the hospital—and will probably sell more. This is a problem many families have which can be a terrifying experience for both parents and children. Another problem of prime interest right now is the question: Are teens really that hard to understand? One student mother said, "No, they are not hard to understand, you just have to take the time,"—this sold several times. And her teen-age daughter sold "How to Handle Parents" to a teen-age magazine. Practically anything else in this line, from how you explain advanced religious concepts to children, to how do you teach a child not to talk to strangers to how to instill discipline in your child and many other family topics, make good articles.

10. *Confessions:* When we think of confessions we usually think of confession magazines. But there is a good article field in just confessing about your problems and how you solved them. Here are a few examples:

1. "I Was a Teen-age Dope Addict."

2. "I Drove My Husband Away."

3. "My Children Were Driving Me Nuts."

Now make your own list and see what you come up with.

11. *The New and Unusual:* Glance through your local newspaper every day and within a month, you'll come up with dozens of new things people are doing. Practically all of these can be sold. (Remember, of course, that everything can be sold—it is just a matter of matching the idea to the market.)

For instance, our classes discovered a man who had invented a new type of electronic mouth organ (*Popular Mechanics*), a local professor using a computer to paint abstracts, and a new type of plow (*Farm and Ranch*). In addition, when computer accounting was brand new, we were able to sell articles on this subject to a great many trade magazines. The same was true when the bank card system was in its infancy—practically every retailer in the country wanted to know how it would affect him—this sold over 40 times to a number of different business magazines—finally, when the State Parks started instituting a recreation system, a number of camping magazines picked it up.

12. **Local Organizations:** Active organizations always mean good article ideas.

For instance, a local church sponsoring a two-week summer hiking trip for it's teen-agers down the John Muir trail in Yosemite National Park sold to *Parade* under the title "The Church Hits the Trail," and an organization who gave its single retirees a card to put in the window every day if they were all right sold to the same magazine.

13. *Newspapers Are a Gold Mine:* Newspapers are absolutely the best place to find article ideas. Many writers depend on this source entirely. Others confess that 90 per cent of all of their ideas come from their local newspaper.

In the past we've sold articles to *Redbook, Parade, Family Circle, Field and Stream,* and most others just from newspaper ideas.

Some of the articles that have come directly from newspaper's accounts are "Antitranspirants–How the State of California Sprays Its Oleanders to Keep Them from Losing Water" (*Grounds Maintenance*), a lady who specializes in making dolls (*Retirement Living*), a new steam car, and many articles on Monarch butterflies.

The advantage of the hometown newspaper is that if the stories are local, you can get to your sources easily for both research and pictures. In addition, ideas keep coming daily.

Now how do you do it? Every day go through the local paper and clip out those items that interest you.

At the same time, go through the magazines you'd like to

sell and look at their articles. As you think of the magazine's titles, try to relate them to the ideas you're now running into. If they come close in general category, you may have the basis for an article sale. *Remember, however, an idea is absolutely no good at all unless you find a market for it.*

Just how does this work? Suppose you're thumbing through *Grit* and find a personality piece on a woman who's renovating a Nevada ghost town. In your local newspaper, you read another about a woman starting her own narrow-gauge mountain railroad. The two ideas should immediately tie together since they fall in the same category.

Let's take another example: The science and mechanics magazines, right now, seem to be doing many articles on backyard airplanes—you read about a man with an extremely unusual one—a gong should go off and you should query immediately.

Remember, however, the important thing is not the idea but the market.

Now here's a clipping guide that will help you decide whether your idea is a good one for a magazine or not. In the beginning, you will have to guess a lot. But as you practice this awhile, you will begin to recognize good salable ideas almost immediately.

Select a local news item you think could be expanded into an article for use in a magazine (skip wire stories and syndicated material). Paste the item alongside the questions on page 56 and answer them.

GET ON A REGULAR CLIPPING SCHEDULE

To make sure you have a never ending source of ideas on your way to a big-money income, start a regular clipping program. I suggest using both magazines and newspapers. What you do is go through the local newspaper daily and clip everything interesting—on those you have immediate use for, write queries to editors. On those needing more information, put

1. Is this item similar to anything written about in magazines I have read?

2. Is this a problem that will be of interest to the readers of these magazines? If so, do I think I could tie it in with local statistics, quotes from authorities, etc.?

3. Eliminate the details which have only local interest (names of committees, etc.). Will I have material left which can be expanded into a feature for magazines?

4. What else will I need? What angle will have to be developed?

5. Actually how good is this? Do I think it has a chance of selling?

them in a folder with a possible title and add more information as you find it.

A good example of this is people who get lost in the mountains—a good article would need clippings covering a considerable period of time. After a year or two of clipping, however, you'll be surprised how much of the research is already done.

Magazines should be handled the same way as newspapers. Go through as many as you can get your hands on regularly, clip out those items that interest you. Some of them will give you ideas that you can sell immediately, other clippings will go into your research file where the facts can be used later in your own articles.

KEEP A NOTEBOOK

This is a continuation of clipping. Anytime anything triggers you, by all means jot it down so you can write queries or use it later.

This should include possible ideas—all information you can collect for research—interesting people—or anything else that strikes you.

For instance, suppose you're driving along and see a houseboat sitting in somebody's yard with wheels—unusual, isn't it? Jot it down, plus the address. If the name is on the mailbox, add that too. You probably won't use it immediately but you might later.

In another vein, suppose someone comes to the front door and says to you, "Lady (or Sir), you just won a prize in our contest." Don't feel you're losing time, take out your notebook and listen. A student who did this sold a piece to *Retirement Living* called "The Lucky Winner's Racket."

Maybe somebody says to you, "I sure wish we could find a place to keep our trailer off the street." If this is of interest, take out your notebook and write it down. You may well do a trailer magazine article later on just what to do with your trailer in the off-season.

Everything then, becomes material. The trick is to write down those things that hold a special interest for you.

MARKETING YOUR IDEAS

Ideas (here is where many writers both beginners and semiprofessionals fall down), are easy to find, markets a bit harder. In our classes, however, we've found some shortcuts that really work.

Suppose, for instance, you read in the newspaper that the Monarch Butterfly is coming back to Pacific Grove, California this week and some local college student is going to tag them for scientific study. Now you think this would make a good article but you don't know who would want to buy it.

The first thing we do is try to find what groups of magazines would be interested. In the front of a current issue of *Writer's Market,* you will find a list of the various magazine categories. In the beginning you won't have any idea of which groups take what, but I suggest you spend considerable time going over *Writer's Market,* getting familiar with the many magazines. Then take your subject and run down through all of the categories asking yourself this question, "Will this group of magazines be interested in my idea, and if they would, what angle would they like most?"

We find, in practice, it's important not to be too hasty in saying, "no." Many farm magazines, for instance, have a woman's and family section which takes recipes, fashion, travel, and similar items. The magazines put out by automotive concerns often take travel, driving tips, and many general-interest pieces. The secret is to start becoming familiar with a wide range so you can answer "yes" or "no" intelligently. In the beginning, guess.

There is probably no subject that won't fit at least three categories and most will have eight to 15 possible outlets.

Next make yourself up a list of those that might possibly be interested in your subject. With our Monarch Butterfly idea, for instance, we'll look through these categories:

Animal Magazines
Art Magazines
Association, Club, and Fraternal Magazines
Astrology Magazines
Automotive Magazines

Aviation Magazines
Business and Finance Magazines
Company Publications
Confession Magazines
Crossword Puzzle Magazines
Detective and Mystery Magazines
Farming and Rural Interest Magazines
General Editorial Magazines
Health and Medicine Magazines
Hi-Fi and Music Magazines
History Magazines
Home Service and Garden Magazines
Humor Magazines
Juvenile and Young People's Magazines
Men's Magazines
Military Magazines
Miscellaneous General Magazines
National and World Affairs Magazines
Nature Magazines
Negro Magazines
Newspapers and Sunday Supplements
Photography Magazines
Popular Craft, Science, and Hobby Magazines
Regional and Travel Magazines
Religious Magazines
Science Fiction Magazines
Sport and Outdoor Magazines
Theater, Movie, TV, and Entertainment Magazines
Trade Journals
Western Magazines
Women's Magazines

Then we'll list all groups we think would be interested in the butterfly piece:

Animal Magazines	Regional and Travel
Aviation	Religious
Nature	Outdoor
Farming	Women's Magazines
General	Young People
Fraternal	Newspapers (Sunday mags)
Health	Photographic
House Organs	

Finally, we go through the magazine list under each category and make a yes or no guess. Under nature magazines, for instance, here are the ones we decided might like something on the Monarch:

Audubon	*Frontiers*
Canadian Audubon	*Natural History*
Pacific Discovery	*National Wildlife, International Wildlife*

Every one of them is a possible market—this particular piece actually sold to *Audubon.** We then do the same for all possible categories (animal magazines, aviation, farming, etc.).

Using this same technique with your own topic you'll discover you can come up with many possible markets. As soon as you make your list, start querying. Remember, however, query one at a time in each category. Don't worry that you're suggesting the same subject for many magazines. If you do the rest of the job properly and slant the finished article to the magazine's needs and style—each will be different. Only the broad subject will remain the same.

---

*currently buys very little freelance material

Checking on Chapter 3

An article idea actually consists of a subject and an angle. Don't pick out a broad subject like the racial question and expect that to make an article. You must narrow down to a specific topic. To do this, the simplest way is to start asking questions. The Racial Question: Is a people approach the best? Are we holding the colored people back with too many qualifications? Why do blacks destroy their own neighborhoods? All of these make possible article ideas that will sell.

Article ideas must be important. This means they should take into consideration some of man's basic drives. Some of these are sexual gratification, maternal behavior, hunger-thirst, aggressiveness, self-preservation, flight from danger, self-assertiveness, gregariousness, acquisitiveness, filial, paternal, and prematernal feelings and motives.

Article ideas will bring more money, if they are of vital interest to the reader and offer him something extra—also if they contain more detail than usual that is of real interest to the reader.

Article ideas bring more money if they can be sold many ways. Simply try to figure out all the possible markets for a single idea and ask yourself just what angle of this subject magazine readers will be interested in reading about.

Ideas are all around you. These areas make good places to start: conventions, professions and businesses, homes and gardens, crafts, mechanics, hobbies, outdoor and travel, your health, prominent or interesting persons, experiences, family problems, confessions, the new and unusual, local organizations, and newspapers.

Get on a regular clipping schedule and keep a notebook. Ideas will come rapidly when you start looking for them. To do this, scan the newspaper every day and clip out those items that interest you. In addition, keep notes on everything you see or do that you think might make a good article.

Market your ideas by making a systematic

search of all possible markets through the Writer's Market. Take your idea and go through the magazine categories asking yourself, "Will this group be interested?" When you come up with a possible category list, then go through all the magazines under each possible category, again asking yourself if this market will be interested. Send queries to one magazine from each category that you think might like the article. In the beginning, you'll have to guess. As you gain more knowledge, however, you'll get quite good at picking possible markets in advance.

CHAPTER 4

How to Focus an Idea

It's essential to master "focus" now because it's the key to everything else.

Once you learn to sell, you can make a certain amount of income every year just from that knowledge. If you learn to publicize yourself properly, of course, you can have editors coming to you, and double and even triple your annual income with that one technique alone—but even without mastering the publicity techniques, you're going to make some money.

Without a knowledge of focus, however, you won't sell in the first place—you're literally dead. Of course, a lot of writers learn and apply these techniques as they go along without even realizing it. But in this chapter we're going to learn exactly what they are, how to analyze a magazine to determine its idea slant . . . . and how to practice until you become really good at focusing.

MAGAZINES WANT ARTICLE IDEAS
HANDLED SPECIFIC WAYS

What do you mean by focusing an idea? It means that every editor and every magazine has its own way of approaching a subject so it will appeal to its readers—sometimes magazines take elaborate steps (such as surveys) to find out just what their readers are interested in, then the editor approaches that subject in the way he thinks will best fit his readers' interest.

If this is true, then all we have to do to sell a particular magazine is to figure out just exactly how that magazine wants an idea handled and do it that way. Sounds elemental? It is and yet it's still the reason most beginners fail and why even professionals sometimes don't do the bang-up job they could.

Now, let's look at focusing an idea in the broad view. Think of it first in terms of people coming into your home. If you had a group of housewives in for tea you probably wouldn't talk to them about how to build a bridge—you'd talk naturally about such things as children, homes, maybe current events, the community, etc.

Conversely, if you had invited a group of engineers, you wouldn't talk to them about how to bake a cherry pie.

Sound silly? It is, and yet that's what focusing is all about, simply taking the magazine's readers into account and giving them subjects they're interested in, treated in the way they want them treated.

Now this seems simple enough, and yet I've had students who say they won't approach it that way because it's wrong—

they want to write what *they* want to write. That's fine—as long as they also realize that readers have the right to read what *they* want to read and editors have the right to reject what *they* want to reject.

Now, looking at it broadly, as far as the magazines are concerned, let's take a few general categories. This approach means that an article for *Field and Stream* would probably have something to do with hunting, fishing, and the outdoors since that's the kind of readers they have. Garden magazines such as *Flower and Garden,* of course, want articles on how to raise plants, how to take better care of your yard, etc. This is just general good common sense.

Carrying this a little further, women's magazines want articles of interest to women—such as child raising, family problems, cooking, fashions, and others. Trailer magazines, of course, are interested in articles on trailers and trailer life.

Now, all of this seems elemental and it is—but you'd be surprised how many times writers send magazines subjects that are completely unsuitable.

But focusing an idea means even more than this, so let's take it one step further.

HOW DO YOU FOCUS ON A MAGAZINE'S IDEA SLANT?

Let's look at one particular magazine, with the idea of slanting ideas into that magazine.

In order to do this intelligently, we have to form an idea of what the magazine itself is trying to do. We'll study the California regional edition of *American Home*. This means then, that they will be interested in general articles plus a great deal about California in particular. If you look at the table of contents, you'll see that their articles come under the categories of *homes and maintenance, decorating, foods, kitchens, equipment, home projects, gardening,* and additional features, which relate to the home.

On the front cover a blurb says "For active young home-makers." When you read the magazine you realize that it is aimed at active young homemakers making incomes of from $9000 to about $25,000 a year (a middle-upper income group).

Now, going even further, let's look to the titles of a few articles. Here are: (1) "Quick-Change Acts for Your Home" (how to make simple structural changes to improve your house); (2) "The Fun of Instant Decorating" (using unusual materials to achieve different decorating results); (3) "How to Cook Electronically"; (4) "Create a Carefree Lawn"; (5) "What's Your Liability as a California Homeowner" (what are you liable for and how to be protected).

Practically every article shows you how to do something. Every article is almost a *how-to* in that it talks about something of concern to you as a homemaker—decorating, homes, and maintenance.

Taking this hint, let's see if we can't come up with ideas that would be of interest to this magazine.

Now vacation living, VA and FHA foreclosures, green-houses, selling a house, and zoning are all possible subjects.

It's not enough to just have general subjects, we must also put an angle on it that fits the magazine.

Remember that this magazine basically likes the how-to side of it, so let's see what we can do. (1) If we discuss what's coming in vacation living, in vacation homes and how you, as readers, can select the best value—this would be close. (2) In VA and FHA Housing, we should probably ask the question, "Is this a good buy—and what can you do to get the best value for your money?" (3) With greenhouses, we'd probably want to discuss how to build a convenient backyard greenhouse. (4) And in selling your house, these readers would probably want to know how to get their house ready to sell at the top dollar. All on the how-to theme—and all slanted toward that particular audience.

Each one of these articles either my students, or I, have thought up and sold over the past several years to this magazine.

Let's try the same thing again with another magazine, using one particular subject—*overpopulation.*

Now, *Field and Stream* is a magazine for the outdoorsman—hunters and fishermen, family campers, etc.

If we look at a particular issue, we will see such categories in the table of contents as *where to go,* and *how to do it.* All articles, of course, will approach their subject from the point of view of the outdoorsman.

In a particular issue we'll see these titles: "Snowmobile's Buyer's Guide"—"How to Skin a Bear"—"Pesticides Anyone?" (are they endangering our game?)—"Last Minute Buck" (elk hunting in Wyoming)—"Twenty Bass in Spots" (20 places where you can get good bass)—"What's New on the Pacific Flyway?"—"Lightweight Chain Saws" (how good are they for chores around the camp?)—"The Intricate Art of Turkey Calling."

Now, let's take our subject of overpopulation and see if we can fit it into the mainstream of this magazine. Let's start with *overpopulation* itself. That, of course, is much too wide to be of interest as an article for *Field and Stream.* So, let's narrow it a little bit and ask the question, *"Will there be room for everybody tomorrow?"* This is a little better, but it doesn't specifically tie in the interests of outdoorsmen.

Okay, let's narrow it a little further and say *our disappearing park lands*—this is getting better—outdoorsmen are concerned about the disappearing wilderness, but we need a little more—so we'll narrow it even further. Next, let's say *too many people in the wilderness*—this, again, is a subject that really concerns hunters and fishermen, but, it's just a little bit too general to be of real interest.

Now you happen to discover that the Park Service and the U. S. Forest Service are managing the wilderness areas to take care of the growing number of people there. This, then, becomes an article—and one I did for *Field and Stream* under the title "Our Fragile Wilderness" (telling just what the Forest Service and Park Service were doing about the overpopulation in back country areas).

The idea is to take your subject and narrow it down until it seems to fit in with the basic ideas of the magazine. This will take some practice, but after a while, you'll get quite good at it—and when you do, you'll find the magazine saying "yes" regularly.

YOU MUST LOOK AT IT FROM
THEIR POINT OF VIEW

Actually, the subject of overpopulation is a good one for many, many magazines. In order to get an idea angle that will fit a particular magazine, however, we must look at it from their point of view.

So, let's see how some other magazines handled this same subject.

Today's Health (a magazine put out by the American Medical Association) which is concerned with health, the latest in medicine, recreation, and similar items, did an article on overpopulation titled, "130,000 Babies a Day (Is the Pill the Answer?)."

Science Digest tackled it from a scientific angle and called it "The Boom in Birth Control," with many statistics and figures.

Guns Magazine did the same article under the title "Too Many Hunters in the Wilderness."

All of them basically looked at this subject from their own

point of view and came up with an angle which fits what they're interested in.

DIFFERENCE IN FOCUS WITHIN A FIELD

Although you might think that magazines within a general field would tackle the same subject in the same way, this just isn't true. Each editor has his own idea of the way he thinks his readers want to look at a subject—and you have to take this into account.

I find in my classes that it's not wise to assume we know what an editor wants just because we know a little about the field, we have to look at every magazine individually and determine the focus.

Now, in the trailer field, for instance, there are several magazines. If we look at three of them, *Trailer Life, Woodall's Trailer Travel,* and *Wheels Afield,** we'll see some different approaches.

In travel articles you'd think they'd take trailer trips—done in the same way—but this isn't true.

Art Rouse, at *Trailer Life,* more or less likes to stand in the middle of his subject and see what there is to explore. For instance, not long ago he was running a monthly state series that examined everything of interest to travel trailerists within a state.

He also does articles which help you get more out of travel, under such titles as "Have a Travel Target"—pointing out that it's more fun if you have something to do when you get there.

Woodall's Trailer Travel requires detailed pieces that take a large general area and tell quite a bit about it. This can be done in the first person or other ways.

---

*And *Wheels Afield* doesn't use travel articles at all but confines its articles to the technical side of trailering . . . tests, brakes, hitches, etc.

As you can see, each approach is different and unless you have read the magazine and tried to understand its approach, you could miss quite easily.

HOW DO YOU GO ABOUT LEARNING TO FOCUS?

The secret of learning to focus on a particular magazine and get an editor to say "yes" to you time after time isn't too hard, but it's going to require quite a bit of work.

First of all, I find in class that it's best if I make my students go through the magazine looking for nothing but the idea slant. We look over the same areas here as we did in Chapter 2, How to Put the Odds in Your Favor, but this time concentrating on the way a magazine looks at the world (its focus or idea slant), forgetting all else.

Now take the magazine and just look at the cover. In looking at a current copy of *Field and Stream,* I see two hunters with a turkey over their shoulder—this tells us that they like to focus on hunting, fishing, and outdoor details. Then we start leafing through the magazine looking at the ads. In *Field and Stream* you'll see guns, rifle scopes, batteries, Jeeps, chain saws, tents, cars, tire ads, binoculars, boat ads, and much more— after a while, we begin to get an idea of what the reader is like.

We know in looking at *Field and Stream* that this reader is an outdoorsman, that he has quite a bit of money, that he's fairly well read and apparently spends money on good cars, on camping equipment, and on other items.

Then we'll go back and look at the table of contents— again, in *Field and Stream* they seem to stress the categories of where to go—how to do it.

Look at an issue of *Trailer Life* and you'll see the categories of travel trailers, motor homes, pickup campers, do-it-yourself equipment, travel, personalities, subjects of interest to women, and automotive.

This will begin to give you a good idea of the topics taken by that magazine.

But we don't stop here, we now read the letters to the editor. This begins to give us the point of view of the readers and a glimpse of what they'd like to see in the magazine.

In a recent issue of *Field and Stream,* for instance, one letter said: "I would like to compliment Ted Trueblood on the article 'Learn to Think Like the Game.' I would like to say I owe several productive hunting trips to trying to think like what I'm after."

You can see then, that this particular reader likes extremely detailed pieces on the inside of hunting and how to do a better job.

This will begin to give you a clue of what you have to do to come up with an article acceptable to the editor of this magazine.

But keep going—read all the columns and anything the editor has to say—frequently he'll tip you off as to what he likes.

Finally, look at the articles themselves, especially the pictures; see how detailed they are, do they go into the technical side of the subject, do they talk about the recreational side of it or just what? This helps us focus down.

Again, in looking at a recent issue of *Field and Stream,* we see an article on snowmobiles—the pictures show people having fun, then the subtitles talk about safety, clothing, mobility, accessories, competition, and others.

This, then, means that the readers are getting a fairly comprehensive treatment of snowmobiles.

If you were to focus down on a similar subject for their magazine, then you would let the editor know you're going to go into the subject in some detail.

You should do this for every magazine that you want to sell consistently. You'll find after a few tries that you'll begin to understand the focus or the angle the editor wants even better than he does.

(1) Read the titles for a while. (2) Read the editorials. (3) Read the letters to the editor. (4) Look at the titles and subtitles, then pick out subjects and ask yourself just how would *Field and Stream* (or whatever magazine you're interested in) go about doing this and keep at it until you have a real feel. (5) Consider the attitude of the departments.

It may seem simple, and it is—but it's also the one thing that will separate you from the beginner and start you well on your way to becoming a professional writer.

HERE'S HOW TO SHARPEN THIS ABILITY

Whether your goal is to make money writing, or simply to sell consistently, you must sharpen your sense of focus, or "idea slant" until it has a fine edge.

The best way to do this is to practice every chance you get. Take a subject, any subject . . . . then go through six or eight magazines, and after you've looked them over, try to find the angle or focus that idea must take to be suitable for that magazine.

For instance, simply throw out a topic, like Birds . . . . then start tossing out magazines, such as *Field and Stream, Mechanix Illustrated, Baby Talk, Retirement Living, Toys . . .* and others.

The idea from here on is to put yourself in the editor's and readers' shoes and ask yourself what aspect of this subject the readers would want to read about and how it must be presented to satisfy editorial style and requirements.

We know *Field and Stream* is a magazine for sportsmen and outdoorsmen. They do conservation pieces—where to go and how-to-do-it items aimed at the outdoors, fishing ("Bridge Fishing Primer"), boating ("Who Says Propellers Are Obsolete?"), outdoors ("Horse Sense"), etc.

Our article, then, to be properly focused, must be seen through this type of idea slant—possibilities are *how to spot fish through bird habits, looking for live bait*—*watch the birds,* and, of course, we could do *bird hunting, how-to's* (our ideas also would probably have to be put in different words to make effective *Field and Stream* titles).

Now *Mechanix Illustrated* says it is the "how-to-do" magazine and caters to the home craftsman's desire to do for himself. It also provides good science and mechanically oriented articles. Most include information that lets the reader get involved and do it himself. Examples are, "How to Crashproof Your Car," "ABC's of Taking the Misery Out of Moving," etc.

Our focus on birds, then, must take this into account. Possibilities are, "Ten Birdhouses You Can Build," "Novelty Birdhouse for the Backyard," "The ABC's of Getting More Fun Out of Our Winged Friends" (again, we'll probably have to change the titles).

For *Baby Talk,* "Bird Designs for Baby's Room"—*Retirement Living* (the magazine for the retirement years), "Why not Try Birdwatching"—*Toys* (a trade journal), "This Dealer's Sales are for the Birds" .... how a toy dealer uses birds as a giveaway to increase sales.

Pretty far out, aren't they? Certainly a far cry from just sitting down with a subject and doing an article .... and then saying, gosh why won't somebody buy it. They won't because you haven't idea-slanted it specifically for them.

You must now learn this technique backwards and forwards. It is absolutely essential in learning to sell regularly, and certainly so for learning to make big money free-lance writing.

Now, to sum up.

1. All topics must be focused on the slant (how-to, etc.) the magazine is taking and the reader interest.

2. You can find this through study and practice.

3. To get good at this, take any subject and try twisting the angle around to fit a half-dozen diverse magazines.

4. Offbeat ideas are especially welcome, provided they are oriented into the magazine's idea slant .... as a matter of fact, magazines are always looking for different and unusual

ideas . . . . the problem is they must fit the categories, the idea slant, and reader interest. Often you can achieve this desire for the offbeat by taking a way out subject, and twisting the angle until it fits . . . . (in fact, this approach probably would establish you faster with editors than any other).

Checking on Chapter 4

Proper idea focus is essential. This is a must if you're going to hit a wide variety of magazines and put together a big-money writing income.

Magazines want article ideas handled their way. The ideas must meet the magazine's approach and satisfy their readers.

You must focus on one particular magazine at a time. It does little good to do a general article. You must make sure each piece fits the magazine you're going to send it to. To do this, study each magazine in detail, narrowing down, until your approach fits their needs and formats.

Each magazine has a different focus. Even similar magazines within a field require that similar articles be handled in a different manner.

Learn a magazine's focus. You can do this by looking at the cover, article titles, slant of the columns, letters to the editors, table of contents, and advertisements. This is not the same procedure used in trying to decide what kinds of articles they take. Mechanically you go through the same process, but in this case, try to discover how the magazine looks at the world, how they approach each subject . . . . and exactly what their idea slant is.

Finally, pick any subject and a group of magazines at random. Then practice idea-slanting that subject into the magazine until you can do it at ease with any subject and a variety of magazines.

CHAPTER 5

How to Get Facts
and Information

Making big money free-lance writing means learning to handle all parts of writing in such a way as to make your dollar-per-hour rate soar.

This is just as true of research as it is of the writing itself. We must master the information-gathering techniques to such an extent that they become second nature.

Of course, one of the questions asked most by beginners and advanced writers too is just where in the world do I get good, solid information fast?

The answer actually is that facts are everywhere and you should learn to gather most of your material as you go along doing other things.

In addition, you should learn to look in many directions

for information. Don't think of just one source. In a major article it's not enough to interview just one person. You should also try to get printed information, newspaper material on the subject—and much more.

When you finish researching an article and get ready to write, you should have many times more material than you will ever need.

You should also know a great deal about the subject itself at this point—and be able to do additional related articles with very little extra work.

Many times a professional writer will have 30 or 40 pamphlets, ten or 15 interviews, a number of newspaper stories and magazine articles on the subject and much more. Sometimes his file for a 1500-word article will contain literally reams of information.

The trick from here on, of course, is to select just the right information to fit the article you're going to write. However, in this chapter, we want to talk about how to get that information in the first place.

Before you start to research, think about what you are going to do. First of all, just how much do you know about the subject yourself? In many cases there is more in your own background than you realize. Your own experiences, your thoughts on the subject, the experiences of others you know— all may well make valuable article material.

Next, think about what you've read on this subject. Start clipping from the newspaper and everything else you can find. Who do you know around you that can tell you something about the article you're trying to put together. For instance, if it's a medical article, is there a specialist in your town you can go talk to, or perhaps a doctor who can put you in touch with a specialist or tell you where to go for more information?

Think of the government agencies near you that may be able to get you started. If it's an article on some phase of business, perhaps the Small Business Administration can give you places to go for more information. Quite often people you contact first can put you in touch with others who do have the information you need.

Basically what you do is first try to think of all the places you can go—then gather that information and let the names and sources you run into there lead you on to more.

Now, step by step, let's look at specific sources of information and just how you can use them effectively.

USING REFERENCE BOOKS–YOUR LIBRARY
REFERENCE DESK CAN HELP

Sometimes the best way to start your research is with reference work. These may be encyclopedias, *Guide to Periodical Literature,* and others.

1. Encyclopedias.

Actually, encyclopedias are only a starting point. Usually there's not enough information here to give you more than a few basics. But you will find them a good outline of a selective field and the starting point for your subject. The list of references at the end of the article in the encyclopedia will suggest more books and other avenues to pursue. You'll find the *Encyclopedia Britannica* one of the most authoritative and scholarly. The *Americana* is good in the field of applied sciences, businesses, and government and has an American viewpoint. The new *International Encyclopedia* with its new yearbook is valuable for Latin-American biography.

2. Atlases and Gazetteers.

Doing travel articles? Or need some general information on the location of a place? You'll find the *Rand McNally Commercial Atlas, Shepard's Historical Atlas and Gazetteer* extremely helpful. Also, don't overlook the information you can get from gasoline company maps. A lot of writers have collections of these from all 50 states and find them extremely useful when starting research.

3. Biography References.

Doing a personality piece? Or need information on someone as an incidental part of your main article? Then you should know where to go for biographical information. There are a number of reference works here that will help:

(1) *Biography Index*—indexes of biographical material and current books as well as 1500 periodicals. (2) *Dictionary of American Biography*—listings of dead Americans who have made some significant contribution. (3) *Dictionary of National Biography*. (4) *The National Cyclopaedia of American Biography*. (5) *Webster's Biographical Dictionary*. (6) *Who's Who*—you'll find a whole *Who's Who* series that'll be extremely helpful. First there's *Who's Who* published annually in England, *Who's Who in America,* and many others, such as *Who's Who in American Education, Who's Who in Art, Who's Who Among the Clergy, Who's Who in Medicine, Who's Who in New York, Who's Who in the Theatre,* and others. (7) Miscellaneous biography—finally, don't overlook such useful sources as *Twentieth Century Authors, American Authors, Dictionary of Music and Musicians, Scientific Encyclopedia, Dictionary of American History, American Men of Science, Congressional Directory, Leaders in Education.*

4. Periodical Indexes, Writer's Goldmines.

This is a good place to start any article—every month what's been published in many magazines and periodicals is indexed in one way or another—and is just waiting for you. Since facts aren't copyrightable, you'll be able to use much of this material for research and as a jumping off place to contact authorities in the field.

Now, here are a few you should know about: (1) *Readers' Guide to Periodical Literature*—this indexes a selected group of major magazines each month and should always be the starting place. Never query a major magazine until you check the *Readers' Guide to Periodical Literature* to see what's been done, (2) *Index to Periodical Literature*, (3) *Social Sciences & Humanities Index*, (4) *Magazine Subject Index*, (5) *The New York Times Index*, (6) special indexes your library can get for you devoted to agriculture, art, biology, chemistry, drama, education, engineering, law, industrial arts, internationalism, public affairs, psychology, and others.

5. Miscellaneous Reference Books.

There are many more reference books which can be extremely useful in your research—the more you go through, the more complete your research will become. Here are a few others: (1) *Monthly Catalog of U.S. Government Publications.* This is the latest and most accurate government information on almost any subject you can imagine. (2) *Famous First Facts* (Joseph N. Cane) records, events, discoveries, and inventions in the U.S. in both chronological and geographic indexes. (3) *Guide to Reference Books*—published by the American Library Association. (4) *John Minnow's Reference Books* (only English books). (5) *Subject Guide to Books in Print* (this will give you an index to the books published by subject matter—another good place to look for information), also *Paperback Books in Print.*

THE LIBRARY

Probably one of the most valuable tools any writer has is the library. By using the library you don't have to live in cities of New York, Philadelphia or others—in fact, living in the country is almost as good as anywhere else.

Of course, the better your library, the more you have to work with. Some have good historical sections, special departments, and sections that will enable you to do very specialized research. Many writers in the past have, however, done complete books without ever leaving their home town. Marchette Chute, for instance, wrote her biography of Shakespeare of London without ever leaving home.

First, of course, you'll want to go to the library card file and look up the subject matter you're interested in. Actually, however, this is just the beginning. From here on your librarian can really help.

In actuality, a librarian can make or break a writer as far as research is concerned. They know where items are you don't dream exist and can find information for you that they've run across long before.

By all means, then, take librarians into your confidence—get as well acquainted with them as possible—and tell them what you want and need. You'll be surprised what pamphlets, books, and other information they'll save for you from time to time—and sometimes they'll even send for books they've read about in newspapers and magazines, just so you will have a chance to look at the material.

When you begin to get your library material together, however, your job is just starting. One writer I know then takes his subject, goes through each book or the piece of material, and puts the items on 3 × 5 file cards.

For instance, James Cerruti—in doing a book on animal sex—happened to stumble on a book on animal psychology.

He went through and abstracted everything that had to do with animal sex out of the book and his other reading.

His file cards came out looking like this:

Card 1: females who kill or lure males to death—ancentrophus—only females are aquatic. Their scent lures males over water.

Card 2: erotic smells, musk deer. Has supplied humans with perfume thus inviting annihilation (note, is there an absolute sexy smell that works on both deer and us in the same way?) among animals and goats. Urinate on own heads to intensify sexy odor; sometimes goats blind self and have to be slaughtered.

As you can see, when you're through you will come up with literally hundreds of file cards with information like this.

The trick then, is to shuffle your cards into piles illustrating general topics—and go from there.

NEWSPAPER LIBRARIES

One of the most useful sources for any writer—and one I have used many times—is the local newspaper library. In many cases, your newspaper keeps clippings of everything appearing in their columns of a local nature.

The San Jose Mercury-News, for instance, clips everything to a paper backing and puts it in their files by subject.

You can then go to these files, request the subject, and get whatever they've done.

Suppose, for instance, you want to know about a local politician. In researching material on this subject, I simply went into the paper and asked for anything they had. The pile I got was voluminous. This particular time they were even good enough to let me bring in a typewriter and copy the material right there.

Your regular library, too, often will have microfilm copies of some of the big-city newspapers. This again will prove extremely helpful.

THE GOVERNMENT

There's a vast storehouse of material here just waiting for you. No matter what your subject, somebody in the government has some information on it—many times I've sent to a government office for a few facts and received literally a box of pamphlets and other material. In addition, the government can often supply pictures on particular subjects.

One of the best sources of information from the government is the Superintendent of Documents, Government Printing Office, N. Capitol and H Sts. N.W., Washington, DC 20401.

You can get a list of material being published monthly by sending for the monthly catalog of United States Public Documents.

In addition, you can get on the list of Selected List of United States Government Publications—this is free and comes to you every month.

This will give you a good idea of some of the many places you can get information from the government.

In the past, I have done many articles using almost nothing except this material.

For instance, one day I noticed in the list of Selected Publications that came across my desk a reference to a pamphlet of Recreational Opportunities on Indian Lands. I sent for this at a cost of about 35 cents and subsequently did many articles from it.

First, I did an article for George Wells at *Camping Guide Magazine* called "Camping with the Indians." Here we went into all the camping possibilities on Indian reservations—then George called me and said this was a great idea for other magazines.

So we sat down and put together a list of magazines we thought would be interested in this article. As a result, articles on recreation on Indian lands appeared in *McCalls, Argosy, Trailer Life, Sports Afield,* and several other magazines.

Although it required some trips and phone calls to fill in the information, the basic facts came from one government publication.

Glance through any selected list of government publications, and you will see the wide variety of subjects they offer. Here's a few:

(1) Conservation Plantings Invite Birds to Your Home.

(2) The Nature, Ecology, and Control of Canadian Thistle.

(3) Vital and Health Statistics—On the Population by Household.

(4) Comprehensive Mental Health Planning.

(5) Light List Volume III—Pacific Coast and Pacific Islands—The Lights a Mariner Needs for Navigation.

This is just a sampling from one bulletin. Each one contains from 50 to 60—all providing a gold mine of material if you're interested in that particular subject.

Besides this, the U.S. Government puts out a *U.S. Government Organizational Manual* which you can obtain from the Superintendent of Documents.

This lists all the organizations of the government, including all bureaus and other offices under each department.

Every department that has anything to do with a subject you're interested in can provide you with a great deal of information. You can also get quotes from authorities and heads of departments—and often they'll even review your manuscript for you.

What I do when I'm starting research on any project is to take the *U.S. Government Organizational Manual,* sit down and decide what departments, bureaus, or offices will have some material dealing with my subject, then I write them and ask for general information.

For instance, suppose I was going to do an article on retarded children.

I would first pick up my *Government Organizational Manual* and go through and see how many departments I could find that would have something to do with this subject. Looking through, I know that the Library of Congress would have something on this subject. Perhaps the Surgeon General of the Army would have something on this pertaining to Army dependents, so I put it down—the same is true of the Navy Bureau of Medicine and Surgery. While this may be an outside chance, it never hurts to see. The Bureau of Census also might be able to provide me with statistical information in one form or another —and, of course, the Department of Health, Education, and Welfare.

Then I would try to figure out offices under this last department that might be able to give me additional information. For instance, I would probably also write to the Public Health Service in general, then the Institute of Mental Health under the National Institute of Health and the National Library of Medicine. I would probably also write to the Children's Bureau under the Welfare Administration to see what they could provide. From these I would probably find other offices I could write to in the government, and by this time would be receiving a flood of literature.

When I get down to my final phase of research, I will then write to specific people mentioned in the bulletins for information and ask them for direct quotes. This way I have good material that I can use from authorities in the field.

In addition to this, there are several other ways in which the government can be helpful. Each committee or subcommittee of Congress holds hearings on particular subjects. Each one of these also puts out minutes of their meetings and will be glad to put you on the mailing list. Here you'll find many statistics, quotes from national authorities, and much more. In the past, I have done many articles from this source alone.

For instance, the subcommittee on aging once held quite a number of hearings on fraud (in connection with retirees).

Each month I would receive the minutes of these hearings and a tremendous number of details.

Out of this I did an article for *Retirement Living* magazine called "Exposed Land Frauds"—practically everything in the article came out of the subcommittee hearings. I had quotes from the Attorney Generals of several states—good quotes from the head of the Better Business Bureau, quotes from Senators and other officials, and much more.

In addition they also reprinted a number of magazine articles from which I was able to get more facts.

Finally, the *Congressional Record* can also be extremely helpful. You can get on the mailing list for this (at about $36 a year) by writing the Superintendent of Documents.

The *Congressional Record* is a source of information on what our political leaders in Congress are saying and doing— there is much put in here about things that are going on all over the country—and best of all, you're often able to use some Congressman or Senator for a good quote.

STATE AGENCIES

In addition to the Federal Government, there is much material you can get from the agencies in your own and other states. I have used these many times as article information sources.

Do you need to know something about consumers, credit, or similar items? Many states have a consumer council that will give you this information. What about land frauds or other frauds within a particular state? Sometimes you can get some of this from the state Attorney General. What if you're doing an article on jobs available in the great outdoors—state departments of forestry will help.

And what about travel? Every state has an agency responsible for giving out travel information and in many cases will provide all the material you need.

Not long ago I needed some information on fraud within small governmental districts for an article in *American Home* (California edition), this came from the office of the state Attorney General.

Then *Trailer Life* asked me to do a series of articles on the State Park system. For this I simply sent 50 letters to the director of the State Parks in every state, and the information immediately started rolling in.

In practice, when I need to know which state agency to write, I call the library and ask them to read me the names of the state agencies in the state I'm interested in (usually from the phone book). I then select the one that's most appropriate and direct my inquiry there.

Where to Write for State Travel Information

ALABAMA—Bureau of Publicity and Information, State Highway Bldg., Montgomery, AL 36130.

ALASKA—Alaska Division of Tourism, Department of Economic Development, Pouch E., Juneau, AK 99811.

ARIZONA—Arizona Office of Tourism, Rm. 501, 1700 W. Washington St., Phoenix, AZ 85007.

ARKANSAS—Arkansas Department of Parks and Tourism, 149 State Capitol Bldg., Little Rock, AR 72201.

CALIFORNIA—The Redwood Empire Association, 476 Post St., San Francisco, CA 94102.

COLORADO—Travel Marketing Section, Colorado Division of Commerce and Development, 500 State Centennial Bldg., 1313 Sherman St., Denver, CO 80203.

CONNECTICUT—Tourism Promotion Service, Connecticut Department of Commerce, 210 Washington St., Hartford, CT 06106.

DELAWARE—Delaware State Visitors' Service, Division of Economic Development, 630 State College Rd., Dover DE 19901.

DISTRICT OF COLUMBIA—Washington Area Convention and Visitors' Bureau. 1129 20th St. NW, Washington, DC 20036.

FLORIDA—Division of Tourism, Florida Department of Commerce, 107 W. Gaines St., Tallahassee, FL 32304.

GEORGIA—Tourist/Communications Division, Bureau of Industry and Trade, Box 1776, Atlanta, GA 30301.

HAWAII—Hawaii Visitors' Bureau, Box 8527, Honolulu, HI 96815.

IDAHO—Division of Tourism and Industrial Development, Rm. 108, State Capitol Bldg., Boise, ID 83720.

ILLINOIS—Illinois Office of Tourism, Department of Business and Economic Development, Rm. 1100, 205 W. Wacker Dr., Chicago, IL 60606.

INDIANA—Tourism Development Division, Indiana Department of Commerce, Rm. 336, State House, Indianapolis, IN 46204.

IOWA—Travel Development Division, Iowa Development Commission, 250 Jewett Bldg., Des Moines, IA 50309.

KANSAS—Tourist Division, Kansas Department of Economic Development, 6th Floor, 503 Kansas Ave., Topeka, KS 66603.

KENTUCKY—Division of Advertising and Travel Promotion, Capitol Annex, Frankfort, KY 40601.

LOUISIANA—Louisiana Office of Tourism and Promotion, Box 44291, Capital Station, Baton Rouge, LA 70804.

MAINE—Maine Publicity Bureau, 3 St. John St., Portland, ME 04102.

MARYLAND—Division of Tourist Development, Department of Economics and Community Development, 1748 Forest Dr., Annapolis, MD 21401.

MASSACHUSETTS—Division of Tourism, Massachusetts Department of Commerce and Development, 100 Cambridge St., Boston, MA 02202.

MICHIGAN—Michigan Travel Commission, Box 30226, Lansing, MI 48909.

MINNESOTA—Tourism Division, Minnesota Department of Economic Development, Hanover Bldg., 480 Cedar St., St. Paul, MN 55101.

MISSISSIPPI—Travel and Tourism Department, Mississippi Agricultural and Industrial Board, 1504 Walter Sillers Bldg., Jackson, MS 39205.

MISSOURI—Missouri Division of Tourism, Box 1055, Jefferson City, MO 65101.

MONTANA—Travel Promotion Unit, Montana Department of Highways, Helena, MT 59601.

NEBRASKA—Division of Travel and Tourism, Nebraska Department of Economic Development, Box 94666, Lincoln, NE 68509.

NEVADA—Tourism Division, Department of Economic Development, Capitol Complex, Carson City, NV 89701.

NEW HAMPSHIRE—New Hampshire Office of Vacation Travel, Box 856, Concord, NH 03301.

NEW JERSEY—Division of Travel and Tourism, Department of Labor and Industry, Box 400, Trenton, NJ 08625.

NEW MEXICO—Tourist Division, Department of Development, Bataan Memorial Bldg., Santa Fe, NM 87503.

NEW YORK—Travel Bureau, New York State Department of Commerce, 99 Washington Ave., Albany, NY 12245.

NORTH CAROLINA—Travel Development Section, North Carolina Department of Natural and Economic Resources, Box 27687, Raleigh, NC 27611.

NORTH DAKOTA—North Dakota Travel Division, State Highway Department, Capitol Grounds, Bismarck, ND 48401.

OHIO—Ohio Office of Travel and Tourism, Department of Economic and Community Development, Box 1001, Columbus, OH 43215.

OKLAHOMA—Tourism Promotion Division, Oklahoma Tourism and Recreation Department, 500 Will Rogers Bldg., Oklahoma City, OK 73105.

OREGON—Travel Information Section, 101 Highway Bldg., Salem, OR 97310.

PENNSYLVANIA—Pennsylvania Bureau of Travel Development, Pennsylvania Department of Commerce, 206 South Office Bldg., Harrisburg, PA 17120.

RHODE ISLAND—Tourist Promotion Division, Department of Economic Development, 1 Weybosset Hill, Providence, RI 02903.

SOUTH CAROLINA—Division of Tourism, South Carolina Department of Parks, Recreation, and Tourism, 1205 Pendleton St., Columbia, SC 29202.

SOUTH DAKOTA—Division of Tourism, Joe Foss Bldg., Pierre, SD 57501.

TENNESSEE—Tennessee Tourist Development Division, 1028 Andrew Jackson Bldg., Nashville, TN 37201.

TEXAS—Texas Tourist Development Agency, Box 12008, Capitol Station, Austin, TX 78711.

UTAH—Utah Travel Council, Council Hall, Capitol Hill, Salt Lake City, UT 84114.

VERMONT—Vermont Travel Division, Agency of Development and Community Affairs, 61 Elm St., Montpelier, VT 05602.

VIRGINIA—Virginia State Travel Service, 6 N. 6th St., Richmond, VA 23219.

WASHINGTON—Travel Development Division, Department of Commerce and Economic Development, General Administration Bldg., Olympia, WA 98504.

WEST VIRGINIA—Governor's Office of Economic and Community Development, Travel Section, Rm. B-504, Bldg. 6, Charleston, WV 25305.

WISCONSIN—Division of Tourism, Department of Business Development, 123 W. Washington Ave., Madison, WI 53702.

WYOMING—Wyoming Travel Commission, Frank Norris, Jr., Travel Center, Cheyenne, WY 82002.

TRAVEL INFORMATION FROM CONVENTION BUREAUS AND CHAMBERS OF COMMERCE

Actually, these sources are good for more than just travel articles—sometimes they can give you convention information—and even get the speeches of each speaker. Basically, however, I use these sources for information on the city, or the state, or the local area.

Chambers of Commerce often have good maps. They can also supply you with a list of motels, additional information on the sizes of nearby lakes, historical information, and many, many other facts. This is one of the first places I start with when doing travel pieces.

For instance, I have done many articles on the Ouachita Mountains of Arkansas. I have been there only once, but I got out a map of the state of Arkansas, picked out a dozen towns in the area, and wrote to the Chambers of Commerce. Out of this I received enough pamphlets to do several complete articles.

Now, here's a selected list of convention bureaus that will help you with information on their area:

(1) Cleveland Convention and Visitors' Bureau, Inc.
511 Terminal Tower
Cleveland, OH 44113

(2) Columbus Convention and Visitors' Bureau
Suite 2540, 50 W. Broad St.
Columbus, OH 43215

(3) Greater Boston Convention and Tourist Bureau, Inc.
900 Boylston St.
Boston, MA 02115

(4) Chicago Convention and Tourism Bureau
Rm. 2050, 332 S. Michigan Ave.
Chicago, IL 60604

(5) Metropolitan Detroit Convention and Visitors' Bureau
Suite 1905, 100 Renaissance Center
Detroit, MI 48243

(6) Greater New Orleans Tourist and Convention Commission
334 Royal St.
New Orleans, LA 70130

(7) New York Convention and Visitors' Bureau
90 E. 42nd St.
New York, NY 10017

CELEBRITIES WILL HELP

Do you think you need quotes from celebrities—stars like Bob Hope, Sammy Kaye, Eddie Fisher, and others? If you do, it's quite possible to get these from celebrities' press agents—and it can definitely enhance your material.

Some writers make a specialty of doing articles based on quotes or other information from celebrities. One recently had the idea of asking eight vocalists what their favorite popular recordings were (Pat Boone, Teresa Brewer, Patti Page, Al Hibler, Sammy Davis, Jr., The Crew Cuts, Gogi Grant, and the Four Lads). This was the idea—he had his celebrities, then he got the article approved by an editor, and finally wrote to their press agents. The letters were typed individually, telling each press agent about the idea, what magazine, and what he wanted, plus photographs—this was followed with phone calls. Within two weeks he had the information back from all eight celebrities and was able to do the article easily.

The celebrity press agent, of course, is paid to get his client in newspapers and magazines—and he'll be glad to cooperate with you in most cases.

Here are some of the rules: (1) let the agent know what publication the material is for (or intended for); (2) put a deadline on when you need the material; (3) follow up with a phone call.

In your letter, don't be general—be specific. If you need particular questions answered, ask them—this businesslike approach will get you many more replies than any other.

Now here is a list of general public relations agents:

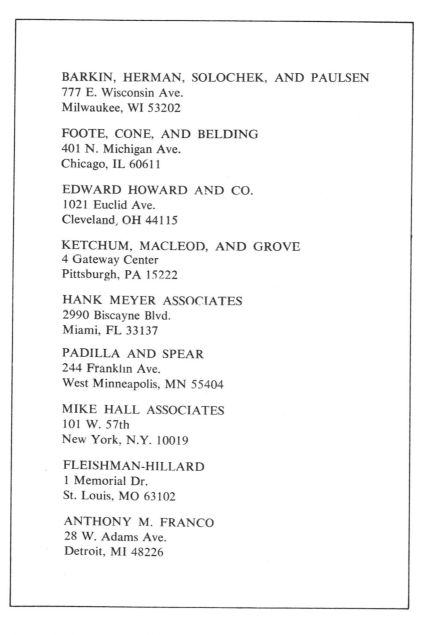

BARKIN, HERMAN, SOLOCHEK, AND PAULSEN
777 E. Wisconsin Ave.
Milwaukee, WI 53202

FOOTE, CONE, AND BELDING
401 N. Michigan Ave.
Chicago, IL 60611

EDWARD HOWARD AND CO.
1021 Euclid Ave.
Cleveland, OH 44115

KETCHUM, MACLEOD, AND GROVE
4 Gateway Center
Pittsburgh, PA 15222

HANK MEYER ASSOCIATES
2990 Biscayne Blvd.
Miami, FL 33137

PADILLA AND SPEAR
244 Franklin Ave.
West Minneapolis, MN 55404

MIKE HALL ASSOCIATES
101 W. 57th
New York, N.Y. 10019

FLEISHMAN-HILLARD
1 Memorial Dr.
St. Louis, MO 63102

ANTHONY M. FRANCO
28 W. Adams Ave.
Detroit, MI 48226

COMPANIES AND TRADE ASSOCIATIONS
MAKE GOOD PLACES TO START

One of the best sources of article information is companies whose business has something to do with your article.

For instance, whenever I do articles on mobile homes, I write to half a dozen mobile home manufacturers for information—if I were doing an article on pipes I would write to pipe manufacturers. The same is true of manufacturer associations. A few years ago when I was doing an article for *Retirement Living* on travel trailers, I wrote to the Trailer Coach Association in Los Angeles—from them I got enough material to do several pieces.

When asking for information, simply write to the advertising or public relations department, tell them what you need, what magazine it's going in, and anything else you feel is important.

Now here are a few selected associations and manufacturers where you can obtain information—you can get a complete list of manufacturers by calling the library and having them look up the names of manufacturers under the category you're working on in the *Thomas Register*. They can also supply you with a list of associations.

Associations and Manufacturers:

(1) *Adult Education*—Adult Education Association of the U.S.A., 810 18th St., NW, Washington, DC 20006

(2) *Aircraft*—The Boeing Co., Corporate Public Relations Director, Box 3707, Seattle, WA 98124

(3) *Aircraft and Missiles*—Northrop Corp., Public Relations Dept., 1800 Century Park E, Los Angeles, CA 90067

(4) *Atomic Energy*—Nuclear Regulatory Commission, Office of Public Affairs, Washington, DC 20555

---

(5) *Automobiles*—Automobile Information Council, 18850 Telegraph Rd., Southfield, MI 48038

(6) *Boating*—National Association of Engine and Boat Manufacturers, Box 5555, Grand Central Station, New York, NY 10017

(7) *Cotton and Cotton Products*—National Cotton Council of America, 1918 N. Pkwy., Memphis, TN 38112

(8) *Family Relations*—American Institute of Family Relations, 5287 Sunset Blvd., Los Angeles, CA 90027

(9) *Farming and Machinery*—Sperry Rand Corp., Manager Corporate News Services, 1290 Avenue of the Americas, New York, NY 10019

(10) *Finance*—American Institute of Banking, 1120 Connecticut Ave. NW, Washington, DC 20036

(11) *Forestry* National Forest Products Association, 1619 Massachusetts Ave. NW, Washington, DC 20036

(12) *Fur*—Fur Information & Fashion Council, 101 W. 30th St., New York, NY 10001

(13) *Gems*—Gemological Institution of America, 11940 San Vincénte Blvd., Los Angeles, CA 90049

(14) *Glass*—Libbey-Owens-Ford Co., 811 Madison Ave., Toledo, OH 43695

(15) *Lumber and Wood Products*—Georgia-Pacific Corp., 900 SW 5th Ave., Portland, OR 97204

(16) *Nutrition*—National Dairy Council, Manager Nutrition Information, 6300 N. River Rd., Rosemont, IL 60018

(17) *Plastics*—Union Carbide Corp., Public Relations Dept., 270 Park Ave., New York, NY 10017

(18) *Photography*—Eastman Kodak Co., Public Relations Dept., 343 State St., Rochester, NY 14650

(19) *Radar*—Sperry Rand Corp., Manager Corporate News Services, 1290 Avenue of the Americas, New York, NY 10019

(20) *Railroads*—Atchison, Topeka and Santa Fe Railroad, 80 E. Jackson Blvd., Chicago, IL 60604

(21) *Recreation, Bicycles, Boating Equipment*—AMF Inc., 777 Westchester Ave., White Plains, NY 10604

(22) *Science and Industry*—Westinghouse Electric Corporation, Photo and TV News Bureau, Gateway Center, Westinghouse Blvd., Pittsburgh, PA 15222

(23) *Shipping*—Matson Navigation Co., 100 Mission St., San Francisco, CA 94105

(24) *Telephone History*—American Telephone and Telegraph Co., 195 Broadway, New York, NY 10007

(25) *Tractors, etc.*—Caterpillar Tractor Co., News Service, Advertising Division, 100 NE Adams St., Peoria, IL 61629

(26) *Wine*—Les Amis du Vin, 2302 Perkins Place, Silver Spring, MD 20910

PUBLIC RELATIONS AGENCIES MAKE GOOD SOURCES

Many times you'll find public relations agencies can be quite helpful in your quest for research material. Public relations agencies, of course, represent many clients and whenever possible they want to publicize their clients. Therefore, they can give you a great deal of help.

Good public relations agencies, I find, are veritable storehouses of story ideas where they have active clients—normally they can also supply you with many facts and story angles.

In addition, because of their close association with a particular client, they can give you many hard-to-get facts and often have printed material.

Also, they can be the door opener between you and the company.

Some agencies do nothing but help get magazine articles and books into print for their clients. For this reason, they will work with the writer, they will get him the facts, and in some cases write the first draft for him.

This happened to me a few years ago with Lobsenz, Inc.,

New York. This excellent firm represents the Dutch Bulb Industry, Kelly Services, Travelers Insurance, and more.

I was doing an article on homeowner liability and asked Amelia Lobsenz to help me get the facts. She actually got the material for me from Travelers Insurance and even wrote a first draft—from here I simply took other material I already had from interviews, combined this, and had an article which was much deeper than if I hadn't had any help.

Again, in getting their cooperation, tell them specifically what you want to do, what material you want, and what magazine you expect to place it in.

Often you can get help from local agencies by simply contacting them through your phone book. Here are some others who can probably help:

Bass & Co. Inc.
111 Broadway
New York, NY 10002

Robert W. Bloch
1 E. 57th St.
New York, NY 10022

Ellis Associates, Public Relations
304 E. 42nd St., Suite 304
New York, NY 10017

Richard R. Falk Associates
152 W. 42nd St.
New York, NY 10020

Fox Public Relations, Inc.
342 Madison Ave., Suite 720-A
New York, NY 10017

Woody Kepner Associates Inc.
3361 SW 3rd Ave.
Miami, FL 33145

Ayer Public Relations Services
1345 Avenue of the Americas
New York, NY 10019

Sydney S. Baron and Co.
540 Madison Ave.
New York, NY 10022

Carl Byoir and Associates
800 2nd Ave.
New York, NY 10017

Gibbs and Soell
117 E. 38th St.
New York, NY 10010

Dudley-Anderson-Yutzy
40 W. 57th St.
New York, NY 10019

Gross and Associates
592 5th Ave.
New York, NY 10036

RESEARCH FROM NEWSPAPERS

One of the best places for a writer to do his research is in the newspapers. Here's what I do—every day I go through the local newspaper, clipping out those items that interest me. When I find a subject I think will make a good article, I start a file— then I clip out articles and news stories from newspapers and magazines and pop them in that file. After about six months, I usually have enough to do an article.

When I go through the newspaper and magazine clippings to do the final research, I'll make a note of all the authorities they mention—and all other sources including institutes, associations, or whatever—then I write to these people for additional information—sometimes I will even go out and interview them.

Some time ago I did an article for *Field and Stream* magazine on managing backcountry wilderness areas. In the newspaper clippings from the *Fresno Bee* I got the name of some of the authorities in the country on this subject and then wrote to them for additional material.

The result was an article loaded with facts.

I also did an article many years ago for *Farm and Ranch* magazine on a new type of plow. In the original newspaper clipping they mentioned several university scientists who had seen the plow and were doing reports on it—I wrote to these people at universities all over the country and received their original reports back. Naturally references to these were included in the final article. You, of course, can do the same.

In researching an article for *Family Weekly*, Charles and Bonnie Remsberg first started looking for everything in print on their subject (Should crime victims be paid?), they began with the *Index to Legal Periodicals*, went to the *Readers' Guide*, and also looked in the *New York Times Index*, and the *Index to the Wall Street Journal*.

Next they went through the out-of-town newspapers in the library, looking for stories of violent crimes in which victims had been severely injured. They found 30 possibilities and noted the victims' names, ages, circumstances, and the names of any police authorities mentioned.

They then started interviewing; the local FBI office sent a breakdown of national crime statistics; Northwestern University's Traffic Institute yielded details of California's compensation program; and the American Bar Association's public relations department furnished leads on compensation legislation pending in various states.

They then went back to the newspaper cases and began telephoning. First they called the newspaper in the town where the story came out and talked to the reporter, then police officers, the hospital officials, doctors, social workers, lawyers, and finally the victims. Sometimes they made seven calls per crime.

Locally also, they talked to the Chicago Crime Commission victims, a university professor, and an Illinois legislator pushing for a compensation law. From the legislator's personal file came case histories of 70 persons who had been left destitute.

Although the research for this article involved a number of sources, newspapers provided a great mass of the material and the starting point for much of the research.

YOUR OWN BACKGROUND

Never downgrade the background information you have from your own past. If you've been a farmer, you've got a lot of information about farms and if you've traveled, you know much about traveling. (With travel, for instance, you know what you like and don't like about motels—you know how difficult it is to change a tire while on the road—and much more.) All of this can make up some of the facts of your own article.

I did an article once on what to tell your teen-ager about the family automobile. At that time I didn't have a teen-ager, but I had heard a lot of teen-agers talk about the problems they were having with cars. For instance, I realized that teen-agers had a hard time holding back when other teen-agers challenged them, they had a hard time convincing their parents that they were responsible, and they were unhappy with the entire general attitude of adults.

On the other side, I knew that it was up to the parents to make sure that their teen-agers were responsible—that the parents could teach them some of the right and wrong things to do—and I had some good examples of parents who were quite concerned and took the time to talk to their teen-ager regularly about the car. All of this I put together, got some facts from the local high school, a few more out of the newspaper, and it became an article for *Family Digest*. A great percentage of it, however, was simply things I already knew from experience and observation.

So when you get ready to start your article research, think about what you already know—then try to add a few additional statistics and facts to this to reinforce that knowledge.

MISCELLANEOUS MATERIAL

Besides this, there are many other sources you can use. If you follow the newspapers and magazines regularly you will frequently find mention of booklets on many subjects that you can write for—the "Better Way" section of *Good Housekeeping* is especially good for this. You'll find such things as "Outboard Handling" put out by the Outboard Boating Club of America and others.

PEOPLE WILL SEND YOU PICTURES

Today practically 90 per cent of all articles must be illustrated with pictures. These pictures come from you or from outside picture sources which most editors maintain. You do not have to provide pictures with all manuscripts, but it's a convenience for editors and pays an additional $5 up each. When you provide pictures, you can either take them yourself or get them from other people.

Fortunately there are many sources available. Here are a few:

1. *Professional Photographers*—this is one of the worst because of the price. However, professional photographers have large files you can use ($2 to $6 each) or they'll go out and take pictures for you.

2. *Local Newspapers*—usually you can buy pictures from your local newspaper for varying rates (I have been quoted prices all the way from $3 to $10 for pictures from newspapers.)

3. *Public Relations Firms and Companies*—usually any company will be glad to *give* you pictures concerning their product. Quite often they also maintain large picture files about other subjects. Examples of these are Shell and Richfield Oil.

4. *Government Agencies*—nearly every Government agency has a picture file. Some, like the Department of Agriculture, have

several hundred thousand in their files . . . . all the way from canning pears to raising hogs, to having a picnic.

5. *State Agencies*—most State Agencies have pictures available for the asking.

6. *Trade Organizations*—the Mobile Home Manufacturers Association and others are good sources for pictures. These are usually free for the asking.

7. *Photo Stock Houses*—these picture agencies have a wide variety of photographs available in both black-and-white and color. Cost here is from $15 up to several hundred dollars for one-time reproduction rights.

You should attempt to build a file of these sources. Now here's a detailed list:

PICTURE SOURCES

The American National Red Cross, 17th and E Sts., NW, Washington, DC 20006 — disaster scenes, ARC aid to servicemen, safety, some historical events

American Telephone and Telegraph, 195 Broadway, New York, NY 10007 — telephone history, Telstar, all phases of phone operation

Catholic Relief Services — U.S. Catholic Conference: 1011 1st Ave., New York, NY 10022 — Church, family life, ecclesiastical personalities. Also can get pictures in the Vatican Area

Camera Clix, 404 Park Ave. S., New York, NY 10016 — stock photos — fee

Pfizer Inc., 235 E. 42nd St., New York, NY 10017 — experimental agriculture, people in medicine, pharmaceutical research

Field Museum of Natural History, Roosevelt Rd. and Lakeshore Dr., Chicago, IL 60605 — 100,000 illustrations on zoology, geology, botany — small fee

Culver Pictures Inc., 660 First Ave., New York, NY 10016 — stock photos — fee

Galloway, Ewing, 342 Madison Ave., New York, NY 10017 — stock photos — fee

General Dynamics Corp, Pierce Laclede Ctr., St. Louis, MO 63105 — military aircraft, missiles, etc.

Library of Congress, 10 1st St. SE, Washington, DC 20540 — material dating from 15th Century, catalogue available

The Nat'l Archives and Records Service, 8th & Pennsylvania Ave. NW, Washington, DC 20408 — War from seized enemy records, particularly World War II, civilian accident investigation

New York Academy of Medicine Library, 2 E. 103rd St., New York, NY 10029 — health illustrations, physicians, hospital, anatomical drawings, small fee

Religious News Service, 43 West 57th St., New York, NY 10019 — clergy and laymen, biblical scenes, 495,000 prints — fee

U.S. Dept. of Agriculture, Photography Division, Office of Governmental and Public Affairs, Washington, DC 20250 — 100,000 black and white pictures of agriculture, conservation, home economics etc.

U.S. Fish and Wildlife Service, Office of Conservation Education, Dept. of Interior, Washington, DC 20240 — black and white photos on wildlife and conservation

U.S. Dept. of Health, Education and Welfare, 200 Independence Ave. SW, Washington, DC 20201 — children at play, pursuing crafts, hobbies, others

Westinghouse Electric Corp., Gateway Ctr., Westinghouse Blvd., Pittsburgh, PA 15222 — science pictures

Wide World Photos Inc., 50 Rockefeller Plaza, New York, NY 10020 — stock photos — fee

Checking on Chapter 5

If you're aiming at big-money writing, you must learn to do your research efficiently. This means gathering material from as many sources as possible and letting other people help you.

Here are the sources writers find extremely useful:

1. *Reference Books.* Use them all if possible. In the beginning, sit down and decide if encyclopedias, atlases, gazetteers, biography references, periodical indexes, or other reference books will help. Then look up the ones you need in the library.

2. *Learn to use the library efficiently.* Try, if possible, to cultivate one particular librarian who will help. In utilizing library information, file cards with brief comments on each item are extremely useful.

3. *Newspaper libraries are helpful.* Many newspapers file everything of local interest. Most allow you to use their morgues or will look up specific material for you. In addition, libraries often microfilm the material from the hometown newspaper and from important national papers like the *New York Times* and the *Christian Science Monitor.*

4. *The government is a gold mine.* Best of all, you can do most of this by mail. Sources are:

    A. Selected United States Government Publications and the *U.S. Government Organizational Manual.* Government pamphlets obtained from the Superintendent of Documents provide much background. You can get more plus direct quotes by writing directly to the departments found in the *Government Organizational Manual.*

    B. Government committees or subcommittees will provide you with detailed information on their hearings. Write to either your Senator or Congressman or one of those on the committee or subcommittee.

    C. The *Congressional Record* can be extremely helpful if you're looking for quotes from Congressmen on particular subjects. You can order this from the Superintendent of Documents or find it in the local library.

5. *State agencies can be as helpful as the Federal Government.* Take your subject, look up the state agencies in the telephone book of the capitol of the state you're

interested in. These can be found in the library for practically all states. Go through the list and decide which agencies or departments might have something on your subject. Then write to these.

6. *Convention Bureaus and Chambers of Commerce can provide travel information and sometimes in-depth information on a city or area.* These addresses can be found by looking up the particular city phone directory you're interested in at the local library.

7. *Celebrities are often as easy to get quotes from as the man next door.* Simply write their press agents and ask a specific question.

8. *Companies and trade associations make good places to start.* Decide which ones would have the information you need and write to several. The local library has directories in which you can find companies and trade associations.

9. *Public relations agencies can be a real help.* Some will even do your research for you. Companies you contact will often put you in touch with their agency. You can also look them up in the phone book.

10. *Newspapers are probably the best source.* They provide a starting point and a place to go. By all means, contact all the names given and go from there.

11. *Your background is wider than you think and the more articles you do on a particular subject, the more useful it will be to you.* After awhile, you'll find you have enough information amassed personally to form a new article, with only a minimum of formal research needed. The secret is to simply start thinking about all phases of your subject, jot down a few notes, and go from there.

12. *Companies frequently put out pamphlets that are extremely useful.* You can find these by watching newspapers and magazines for current ones coming out.

CHAPTER 6

How to Establish Yourself
with Editors

To build a big-money income, try to make yourself indispensable. Sound impossible? It probably is, if you consider indispensable to mean you and only you can do an assignment or a particular group of assignments. But editors do come to depend on writers for certain kinds of articles. For instance, several years ago I did two or three articles on mobile homes and travel trailers for *Retirement Living* (a magazine in the retirement field). I also, at the time, had done quite a bit of work in the trailer field and had a column going in one of the trailer magazines. After the first several articles, the editor called any time he wanted anything related to trailers or mobile homes. In addition, students in my classes have gotten to be "experts" on airplanes, Monarch butterflies, education, nature, and other areas, and find their editors frequently give them assignments when they need something on these subjects. Editors also come to rely on you for coverage in particular geographical locations and will call on you if they know what they want is in your backyard and are sure you can do the job.

Finally, of course, editors will give you assignments simply because they know you will come up with a tight, concise, workmanlike job.

Editors do become dependent on you then for your knowledge in a specialized field, for geographical coverage, and good workmanship. Here is a step-by-step approach which will help you establish yourself in the first place.

ALWAYS HAVE AN ARTICLE IN THE WORKS
FOR A MAGAZINE YOU'RE TRYING TO CULTIVATE

The only real way to build yourself with a magazine is to keep sending acceptable articles. That means a steady, systematic progress toward building yourself as a regular contributor. Once you get an acceptance from an editor, send another query, and get another project in the works. As soon as that's done, start another . . . . keep at it, until the editor knows your work and comes to rely on you for solid material.

Let me show you how this works: I have one student who has sold probably 200 articles, no more than two to the same magazine . . . . Every time he does a story he has to initiate the idea, write the query, and do the article. I have another student who has sold only about 30 articles, but all of them have been to two magazines. Once he finishes one project for his magazines he starts another. As a result both editors have come to know him well. Eighty per cent of his articles are on assignments and often when one of the editors has an idea he picks up the phone and assigns this writer to do it. Last year he was flown to the Pacific Northwest, Florida, and several other areas to do articles that the editor originated—all because he kept at it until the magazine knew his work, liked it, and considered him almost staff. From here on, to build a really good income, all this writer has to do is continue the process until he has 20 or 30 magazines that depend on him as a regular.

The process is quite simple. Once an editor says yes, suggest another project. When that one's sold, start another, until you're selling the same magazine at least six articles a year or more (about half this for major magazines).

SUGGEST IDEAS REGULARLY—EDITORS DON'T KNOW WHAT THEY WANT UNTIL YOU TELL THEM

Sounds strange? Well, it isn't. Time and time again editors will give you an assignment when you suggest it first. They may be looking for something in that particular field, but they're not sure exactly what.

If you show them how this idea will help their readers and how it should be put together, however, you'll often get the job of doing it. And the more ideas you send across their desk, the more work you'll have.

Some time ago I sent *Home and Auto* magazine an idea suggesting a camping merchandising roundup—the reply back simply said, "This is a godsend, we've been trying to decide what to do."

In another instance, *Motor* magazine rejected my original idea but gave me another assignment and asked if I'd be interested in becoming West Coast Editor—all because I sent them ideas and made them realize that I was there and could do the job.

You'll find the more ideas you suggest the more go-aheads and assignments you'll get, simply because the editor keeps seeing your name.

Let's take an example: suppose, for instance, you do articles on child care and you've managed to make a sale or two to *Family Circle*. Now you want to build that market. You can do it effectively with good ideas.

First let's keep in mind what they've done on the subject. Here are some recent topics:

1. How Do We Look to Our Children?
2. How to Achieve Parent Power.
3. What Makes Children Cheat?
4. Who Kills Your Children's Creativity?
5. Olympic Champion Bill Toomey Tells Young People What Winning Is All About.
6. Before and After My Second Child Arrived.

Now we know that to have a good chance your ideas must "more or less" fit this vein, so here's how I'd do it. Maybe I see that someone is talking to the PTA about challenging children with higher and higher goals. That fits the pattern so I'd put it in my idea files.

Then I hear a radio talk about schools holding many children back because teachers place more emphasis on conformity (so the teacher can handle the child) than on curiosity and individual learning. This also goes in the file. Next I pick up the paper and see that a local athlete with a national reputation says that competition is important for children—this is marked down.

Listening, reading, and thinking over the next few weeks, I find three or four more ideas. A psychiatrist asks, "Are children more aware than parents?" A minister tells how to help children grasp complex ideas. A school official talks about parents' responsibility toward kids and cars.

Now I have no idea of whether the magazine will take any of these ideas but I do know that they're close to the pattern and all are solid ideas experts and parents are thinking and talking about. So over a period of time, I will suggest the ones I feel fit best.

TRY TO KEEP TOPICAL

To do this properly, you have to read the magazines. They'll tell you what both editors and readers are thinking about, and you can see what hasn't been covered yet.

Here are some tips to help you do it systematically:

TIP 1. Read the Letters to the Editors and Act on What They Say.

Letters often mention topics readers are concerned about and would like to see in the magazine. If the editor has several requests for the same subject, he's likely to be receptive.

For example, in a letter printed in the "Dear Cosmo" section of a recent issue of *Cosmopolitan*, a reader commenting on an article ("Is Janice Wylie's Real Murderer Still At Large?") stresses that she hopes articles like this will awaken the public to the uses of psychiatry in modern criminology.

This should tip us off to reader interest. And if this is a subject we like and we really want to be topical (as far as the editor is concerned), we should start watching for this type of material.

Suppose, for example, we find a clipping about a psychiatrist working with young men to discover potential rapists. This, of course, should be tried on *Cosmo*.

Then we hear of a local sociologist who advances painting as a way of probing criminal possibilities—again, it becomes a possible topic.

Going back to *Cosmopolitan,* another letter writer tells the editor that she's been taken on occasion by the con game,—Once she bought some "genuine Irish lace" from a door-to-door salesman which practically melted when washed. She discovered it was machine-made in the Orient. She also points out that the article doesn't mention the worst con man of all—the one who takes a girl out a few times, borrows money from her, then disappears. This she explains happened to her twice, once for a lot of money. Other girls she knows have experienced this. Now her rule is "Never lend money to a man."

A sharp writer, of course, would get right on this and offer *Cosmopolitan* some variation of "Loaning Money to Men."

Tip 2. Act on What Editors Say They're Doing.

In a recent issue of *Cosmopolitan,* Editor Helen Gurley Brown talks about the different kinds of anger and also introduces an article on different types of anger and how people respond to them. Taking a tip, we should begin thinking of other ways anger is important plus the effect of different emotions.

If an editor considers anger important to her readers as an article topic, she'd also probably consider the effects of other emotions important. If you're systematic, simply start jotting down a few—hate, jealousy, fear, envy, greed, lust, rage. For instance, how does envy affect people? Can you build it up enough to make a complete article? If so, you might try an outline here.

Tip 3. Keep Files.

If you're seriously interested in establishing yourself at *Cosmopolitan* or any other magazine, you should start a file on each of their article categories you're interested in and clip regularly from the local newspaper. You should also read each article on this subject every month and attempt to come up with something in this category that is topical and a bit ahead of what they've done.

Let's take a sample from the Industry Section. Articles in recent issues have been: (1) "Hello Computers, Goodbye Privacy,"—"1984 Is Just Around the Corner" (subtitle: "The Thinking Machines Know Too Much About Us–The Gossip Along with the Facts") an article about computers and the invasion of privacy. (2) "The Day We All Stopped Breathing"—an article about air pollution. (3) "Credit-Crazed Dolls"—the credit situation; why so many people are so deeply in debt, bankruptcy, and what to do about it.

Looking at these, you will see they are industry or business problems that affect the readers. To lead the editor, you should begin to think about the common industry problems that affect their readers, along with some of the solutions.

Here are a few possibles. In your clipping and reading, you might come up with the fact that builders are jamming us into so little space we're all going to wind up with claustrophobia and an extremely impersonal society.

You also may look at all the new products with yearly models that keep coming on the market and hit on the idea of planned obsolescence—will it drive you to the poorhouse? As you clip in the categories the magazines are interested in you'll find you'll be coming up with many more ideas like these.

THE MORE YOU OFFER A MAGAZINE'S READERS, THE MORE YOU'RE WORTH

Here's how to do it:

An editor of mine once said what readers want most is "take home" value, and that's true. Most readers want to relate articles to their own experiences and use it in some way.

In a travel article, for instance, they'll want to know how much the trip costs, what to see, where to stay or camp, and the dozens of little details that will help them plan their own trip. The more information you give, the better. There are several ways to handle this.

(1) *Give the readers "steps to positive action."* Readers are always looking for ways to do it themselves, one of the ways is to show them how to get in the act. Peter Dickinson, former editor of *Retirement Living* magazine, always tells his writers that one of the essentials of *Retirement Living* articles is "steps to positive action."

These "steps" are simply ways the reader can apply the information.

Here's a sample from the magazine:

> To see South America successfully on your own, you must do your homework thoroughly. You must know the geography in detail, read the guidebooks and study the maps. For instance, keep in mind Quito's famous Ecuador Monument lies near the

airport about 15 miles north of the City. If you visit it by taxi while en route to the airport, it will cost you $1 extra, yet to make a separate visit can easily run $5.

Try to cash your travelers checks at American Express Agencies or Cambios (money exchanges) in capital cities. Banks are miserably slow, while upcountry hotels may deduct as much as 5 per cent for making the exchange. Carry about 25 $1 bills for arrival in each country.

That's one of the ways *Retirement Living* does it—adding this kind of detail to your own article will increase its value to the readers and naturally to the editor himself.

(2) *End-of-the-article guides listing addresses, references, rules, tips, and other items, always add an extra that the reader will really appreciate.* In this "South American" article, *Retirement Living* includes a place to write to for additional information, books to buy for further reading, and extra material that they can get by sending to the magazine itself. Here's a sample concerning where to get additional information on South America:

For information, write: *South American Tourist Organization,* 100 Biscayne Blvd. (Suite 501), Miami, Fla. 33132 . . . *Colombian National Tourist Board,* 140 E. 57th St., New York, N.Y. 10022 . . . *Brazilian Government Trade Bureau,* 551 Fifth Ave., New York, N.Y. 10017 . . . *Panama Government Travel Bureau,* 630 Fifth Ave., New York, N.Y. 10020 . . . *Surinam Tourist Board,* 10 Rockefeller Plaza, New York, N.Y. 10020 . . . *Venezuelan Chamber of Commerce of U.S., Inc.,* 233 Broadway, New York, N.Y. 10005.

RETIREMENT LIVING

(3) *Extra informational boxes help give an article greater value.* The more useful information you can give the reader,

the more valuable that article is going to be. One of the ways to do this is to try to think of all the items a reader will need to know about. Then place that information in boxes which can be inserted in articles. This can be a list of addresses, charts, graphs, tables, and much more.

In the *Retirement Living* article on "South America," there's a box which includes air fares to South America, a box including bus and train links (see sample which follows), and a capsule guide to South American cities. All of these are of great value to the reader and increase the article's real use.

KEEP YOUR NAME BEFORE THE EDITOR

It's a natural rule that editors give assignments to writers whose names are on their minds. The only way you can keep your name on an editor's mind is to either make a name for yourself in a particular area, or keep your name before him at all times. This, I find, is extremely important and is something that nearly always results in additional assignments.

One of my students also believed this and went to great lengths to make sure he kept in constant communication with editors.

In the first place, he sat down once a month and wrote to any editor he hadn't written during the last month. This might consist of a brief suggestion or a note telling about something he'd run into that might interest the editor. He also kept a clipping file on subjects of interest to particular editors, and now and then would put them all in an envelope and send them in. After getting these, an editor would often call and have the writer go out and do an entire article on one of the ideas.

This particular writer also had a picture of himself made up and sent to editors with a note saying, "We've worked together for a long time, now I want you to see what I look like." Again, rather silly, but it did keep his name going across their desks and he did seem to get an extra batch of assignments

Bus and Train Links in South America

	Via	One Way Fare		Via	One Way Fare
Santa Marta—Bogota (Colombia)	rail	$3	La Paz (Bolivia)— Antofagasta (Chile)	rail	$15
Bogota—Cali (Colombia)	bus	$1	La Paz (Bolivia)— Sao Paulo (Brazil)	bus to Santa Cruz, Bolivia, thence weekly rail service	$110
Cali—Popayan (Colombia)	bus	$1.10			
Popayan—Pasto (Colombia)	bus	$2	La Paz (Bolivia)— Buenos Aires (Argentina)	rail	$30
Pasto (Colombia)— Ipiales—Tulcan (Ecuador)	bus	60¢	Antofagasta—Santiago (Chile)	rail or bus	$15-$25
Tulcan—Quito (Ecuador)	bus	$3	Santiago (Chile)— Buenos Aires (Argentina)	rail	$20
Quito—Guayaquil (Ecuador)	rail	$3			
Guayaquil (Ecuador)— Lima (Peru)	through ferry and bus service	$20	Buenos Aires (Argentina)—Montevideo (Uruguay)	overnight steamer (or hydrofoil and bus)	$8.16
Lima—Arequipa (Peru)	bus	$5	Montevideo (Uruguay)— Sao Paulo (Brazil)	bus	$25
Arequipa—Puno (Peru)	rail	$5	Sao Paulo—Rio de Janeiro (Brazil)	bus	$2
Puno—Cuzco (Peru)	rail	$13.30	Rio de Janeiro—Brasilia (Brazil)	bus	$11
Cuzco—Puno (Peru)— La Paz (Bolivia)	through rail and lake steamer	$26.60	fares are approximate and subject to change		

RETIREMENT LIVING

every time a mailing went out. Other writers use some rather ingenious methods to accomplish this purpose (Figure 1).

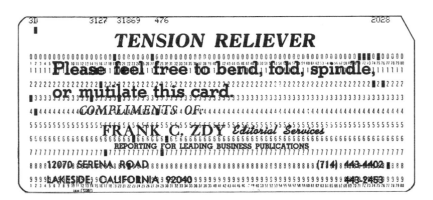

TENSION RELIEVER

Please feel free to bend, fold, spindle, or mutilate this card.

COMPLIMENTS OF

FRANK C. ZDY *Editorial Services*

REPORTING FOR LEADING BUSINESS PUBLICATIONS

12070 SERENA ROAD (714) 443-4402

LAKESIDE CALIFORNIA 92040 443-2453

Figure 1

NOW AND THEN PICK UP THE PHONE

This is just another form of keeping your name before an editor. But it does pay to get on the phone now and then and ask personally about assignments. One business writer budgets $100 a month for this and feels it's important to keep close to what's going on. He's able to keep close to home-office projects this way, and by keeping his eyes and ears open he can offer additional material which will broaden the scope of current projects.

In addition, he makes one trip a year back to New York to talk to these same editors. As a result, he often gets choice assignments editors save for him. He also finds editors come to rely on these trips and often save him editorial slots—including several trips to Europe and South America.

MAKE SURE YOU MEET DEADLINES

There's no more effective way to kill yourself with an editor than to set an article deadline and then miss it. This usually means the editor will have to scramble around for additional material.

If, however, editors come to realize they can rely on you to meet deadlines consistently, you'll find yourself getting many additional assignments and sometimes worked into the magazine almost like a staff member. When this happens life becomes considerably easier.

All of these things are necessary if you're going to make regular, consistent sales that add up at the end of the year to a big-money income.

Checking on Chapter 6

Establish yourself by immediately getting an okay on a new project as soon as you've finished the current one. You can build a solid place with a magazine by selling them articles on a regular basis. Some writers keep ideas in reserve and shoot the next in as soon as the previous project is sold. Six solid sales a year to the smaller magazines and possibly three a year to the majors should be enough to establish you as a regular contributor.

You will build a solid reputation with an editor by offering his readers extras. This should include good, solid, information-packed articles, good steps to positive action, reference material, and boxes packed with extra information he can use.

For instance, in an article on how to obtain part-time jobs, you would include first as many examples, statistics, and quotes from authorities as you find. Then you would show the reader how to get these jobs himself. Next, you might include agencies that could help him and other books he could read. Finally, you might include a checklist of questions he might ask himself before he goes out on the job. All of this would offer the reader extras, increase the article's worth, and help establish you as a solid writer for that magazine.

You can obtain money-making assignments by keeping ideas constantly before an editor. It is possible to find good ideas by checking what the magazine is doing concerning certain topics and offering additional themes in these areas.

It is also possible to obtain good money-making assignments by suggesting ideas you discover by reading letters to the editor, the editor's comments, and from files you build on subjects a particular magazine is interested in.

Always keep your name before an editor. No matter how good a writer is, an editor will tend to forget him, if he isn't reminded of the name now and then. This can be done by sending a newspaper clipping or a short note suggesting ideas regularly.

CHAPTER 7

How to Pick a Specialty

There are dozens of reasons writers give for doing articles all over the map, but from a money standpoint, specialization really does pay. It does for several reasons. First of all, it cuts down on the research.

In interviewing, for instance, you'll know exactly what to ask the interviewee and what exactly you'll need in the way of background material. You'll learn you should look at a celebrity's scrapbook in advance and talk to a number of his friends. You'll also learn how to do this efficiently—often over the phone. Also, you won't ask unneeded questions. In addition, you'll discover a lot of overlap, your interviewee will talk a little bit about another person, and over a period of time, you'll find yourself doing articles on some of these other people. I used to find that a lot of people I've talked to had met Walt Disney personally, and had something to say about him. Although I never did an article on Disney, I would have had some good anecdotes I could have used. The more articles you do, the more you'll find overlap occurring—this is true of all areas. If you start an entirely different field each time, however, none of this will occur.

The more specialized your field is, the more one article hinges on another and the more you can use your research in other ways. In making big money writing, it's absolutely vital that we have all areas working together to produce maximum income in minimum time.

Second, you will be more in demand if you specialize. Magazines like to feel that their writers really know what they're talking about. If you've done ten, 15, or 20 articles on the same subject, they're more likely to trust you to do a very complicated one than they would otherwise. In addition, the more you're known as an expert in the field, the more money you can command in the first place.

MAGAZINES LIKE TO BUY THEIR ARTICLES FROM AN EXPERT

There are several reasons for this—if you've built your name strongly enough as an expert in a field, readers know the name, trust your articles, and are more likely to read them. Magazines, of course, want the greatest readership possible from each article, and will buy you for this reason. In addition, magazines want their articles as authentic as possible. They realize that anyone recognized as an expert in the field can probably handle their articles in a good, authoritative manner.

YOU CAN GET MORE MONEY BY BEING AN EXPERT

Because you are in demand, you will be able to ask for more money than with an ordinary article. If a magazine considers you an expert in a field and wants articles from you, often they will be willing to pay slightly more . . . . 10 per cent or 15 per cent—maybe more. Erle Stanley Gardner told me once that *Popular Science* paid him double their going rates in fields where he was considered an expert, such as houseboating. You may not get double the rates, but you will get some extra money.

WHAT SPECIALTIES ARE THERE?

There are many, many fields in which you can specialize; some, of course, are more lucrative than others. Let's look at a few broad ones:

The Business Field: Just for starters, there are over 2500 business magazines that take articles on how particular businesses have made money in specialized areas. They also buy interviews with industry leaders, general business articles on business problems, roundups, and others.

In addition, the popular magazines buy hundreds of business articles each year. If you are business minded, like business, and enjoy talking to businessmen, this can be a lucrative field. There are many business writers making well above $20,000 a year.

Business articles for major magazines can cover almost any field—for instance, let's take a look at *Cosmopolitan.* Here are a few business titles: "Hello Computers–Goodbye Privacy," "Credit-Crazed Dolls (the credit situation)," "So You Want to Change Jobs (all the different kinds of work available in business)," and others. A basic way to get into this is to send for magazines in fields you're interested in and study them until you think you have some knowledge . . . . build by applying the rules in Chapter 6, How to Establish Yourself with Editors and Obtain Money-Making Assignments.

Science Writing: There's hardly a field more in demand today than science. Pick up practically any magazine and you'll find an article on some phase of science.

You'll also find you have practically no competition. Most scientists and technologists just cannot write popularly. The more educated and the more intense a man is about his subject, the more this seems to be true.

However, the public is looking for more and more pieces

on all phases of science. Even in the popular magazines, you can find articles about agriculture, anthropology, astrology, astronomy, atomic energy, aviation, biology, chemistry, electronics, engineering, geology, mechanics, meteorology, mining, physics, physiology, zoology, jet and rocket propulsion, and a lot, lot more.

The secret of breaking into this field is the same as it is for any other—study the magazines you're interested in hitting, to determine what types of articles particular magazines are taking. Use your local paper, as well as your local college public relations department, to discover possible science articles in your area.

Try to tie possible ideas to markets by going over the articles already done and relating them to your ideas, then query the magazines.

Once you break into one magazine, start making an editor dependent on you by continuing to do work—while at the same time looking for related markets.

Medicine: Here's a field that is just as much in demand as science, maybe even more so. Pick up practically any magazine and you'll find articles such as "New Ways to Cure Your Ulcer," "These Doctors Are Taking the Pain Out of Operations," "How to Live with Your Heart," and more.

There are a number of writers today, such as Lawrence Galton, who make a good living specializing in the medical field. There are magazines, such as *Family Circle,* which carry at least one medical article an issue. Pick up issues of *Better Homes and Gardens* and you'll find the following: "R-X for Animal and Insect Bites," "Why Are You So Tired?," "The Daily Bath, A Few Medical Facts," "When Cancer Strikes Someone in the Family," "How to Handle a Hearing Loss," and others.

It isn't necessary to be a doctor to write these articles, but you must do your homework well, build up an extensive knowledge in this field, and have your articles checked thoroughly (the AMA office in Chicago used to do this—best bet now is a local specialist).

The Food Field: Is this a good specialty? You bet it is. Of course, most food articles in big magazines are staff written, but there are hundreds of smaller magazines buying literally thousands of recipe and food articles every year—in addition, of course, cookbooks are the most consistent sellers today.

Such magazines, as the *Rural New Yorker, Gourmet, Woman's Day, Successful Beekeeping,* and many more, have bought food articles in the past and will buy more in the future.

Building a specialty here means accumulating a library of all possible markets. As a start, go through *Writer's Market* and send for every magazine that takes women's features— don't overlook the religious magazines, the farm magazines, house organs, and others . . . . for cookbooks, examine the category "Cookery" in the subject guide to *Books in Print* in the local library. Scan the titles to give you an idea of what subjects they're taking, which publishers publish this type of book, and the approaches they take.

Automotive: Pick up any popular magazine and you're liable to find at least one article on the car. Look at *Popular Science* or *Popular Mechanics,* for instance, and you'll find a whole category in each issue with such titles as, "Road Racing Big, Big League," "What to Look for in Your New Car," "Saturday Mechanic Rundown on Rubber," and more. A recent issue of *Popular Science* had the "Shocking Facts About Drinking and Driving," "Computer Gives Directions as You Drive," "Four-Wheel Drive Cars Go Anywhere and Fast," and more.

And even in *Cosmopolitan,* you'll find titles like "My Husband Taught Me to Drive," "Right Up the Wall."

Again, follow the old rule of building your library—relate your own experiences to what's being done and query.

Travel: Everyone thinks they can write travel articles, but it's still a good specialty. The market boils down to this—a limited number of travel magazines, *Travel, Holiday, National Geographic;* newspapers, such as the *New York Times,* the *Chicago Tribune,* which buy travel pieces; specialty magazines, which take travel as a related subject . . . . *Trailer Life,*

Camping Guide, Camping Journal, Woodalls Trailer Travel, and others. In addition, practically every magazine publishes some travel articles in the course of a year. Examples of this are: "Hip, Hip, Hawaii" (*Cosmopolitan*), "21 Most Popular Vacation Spots" (*Good Housekeeping*), "The Better Way– Caribbean Cruises" (*Woman's Day*), "Family Vacation Bargains" (*Woman's Day*), and more.

In addition to articles, of course, books make a good travel supplement, and should be considered part of your writing package.

Practically every travel article done today needs a good, solid angle, that explores one facet of a subject in depth . . . . years ago it was quite possible to do "My Trip Through Paris," but not today. Best bet is to take one aspect and explore it in some detail . . . . examples: "Rent a Trailer Through Europe," "The Caves of France" (you'll find a fascinating world here), "Craftsman Hopping Through Mexico" . . . . most articles, of course, now require complete how-to details.

The basics are these: you must know who takes what. Start your own library of every magazine you find that takes travel articles—go through *Writer's Market* looking for magazines that say they take travel and write for copies—whenever you see a magazine you don't know, scan it to see if it takes travel. If so, add it to your library.

After this, the secret is to study the magazines, their angles, what they need, and how they put it together . . . . then offer them exactly this.

Outdoor Recreation: What a field this is. Beginning with the 1950's, outdoor recreation literally exploded into a dozen different facets: recreational vehicles, houseboating, boating, camping, hunting and fishing, water skiing, archery, dunebuggying, trap shooting, backpacking, trail riding, and more.

All of these, of course, had been there before, but most expanded into an all-family activity. Along with it has gone an increase in need.

Today, there are about 100 magazines taking outdoor

articles; in addition, publishers bring out dozens of outdoor books each year—the principal markets for your work are there.

The Outdoor Magazines: These can be divided into the national group such as *Field and Stream, Outdoor Life, Sports Afield,* etc., and the regionals such as *Western Outdoors.*

Guns, Hunting and Fishing Magazines: Most of the gun magazines (such as *Guns and Hunting*), include how-to and technical gun articles on similar material.

Coverage for the fishing group, such as *Sportfishing, Fishing World,* and *Saltwater Sportsman,* includes experiences, conservation problems, and more . . . . in addition, of course, many other magazines still carry some fishing and hunting coverage.

Camping—Recreational Vehicles: There are dozens of magazines which provide articles for campers, trailerists, motor homeowners, camper coach enthusiasts, and others . . . . they use travel, technical articles on recreational vehicles, tents, experiences in the outdoors, and much more.

Boating: Boating is certainly a growing field with such magazines as *Yachting, Family Houseboating, Sea and Pacific Motorboat,* and others . . . . these take the how-to's of equipment, activities (such as skin diving, water skiing), technical material, travel, and more . . . . in addition to the specialized markets, many others carry pieces related to water activity.

Related-Interest Magazines: Such magazines as *Skin Diver, Archery World, Bow and Arrow,* and others cover related outdoor activities . . . . these magazines handle the activity itself, how-to's, technical pieces, personalities, and more.

Conservation Magazines: While not strictly outdoors, such magazines as *National Wildlife, American Forests, Audubon,* and others, do carry conservation and outdoor pieces—most, of course, are strictly related to nature.

Outdoor Books: There are more and more outdoor books being published than ever before, such as *Stackpole's Reading the Woods, Guide to Snow Trails,* and others. To break into this field, it's best to get a number of outdoor articles under your belt, observe who's publishing these books, send for their trade lists, and study what they're doing. After this, if you've got an idea which fits their scope, try a letter asking if they'd be interested, then send an outline and sample chapter.

In addition to these listed, several company magazines, such as *Ford Times, Ford Truck Times, Outdoors,* and others, take outdoor articles. You'll also find outdoor articles in many other magazines—as with all fields, build your own library and study the markets.

Other specialties that get good receptions at magazines include fashions, the family and its problems, education, the race issue, politics, Hollywood, inspiration, health and religion, and much more.

HOW TO MAKE TOP MONEY WITH SPECIALTIES

This isn't hard to do. It's primarily a matter of looking around and seeing what's going on, as well as keeping track of how many writers seem to be in the field, plus application of good-writing business principles. Go through the major magazines and make a list of the fields that reoccur time after time . . . . examples are: health and medicine, family life, education, and others—then begin to observe the writers. For instance, in the medical field, go through 100 issues, make a list of the medical articles, and see how many times the same writers keep reappearing. These most popular fields, with the fewest number of writers, are the ones that pay best and are easiest to break into.

This won't mean that it'll be easy to acquire a good working knowledge—it probably won't, or there would be more writers there. But these will be the ones that the editors will pay a little bit more for. Once you get established, of course, your assignments will be many. As with any phase of writing, you'll never make big money by simply writing one article that pays well. Making big money writing, as we keep pointing out in this book, is a matter of putting many writing business skills together so that the whole approach makes you money.

This means, in addition to learning which fields are in demand, and which ones have the fewest writers, that you must start establishing yourself in the field of your choice. You must start publicizing yourself to make your work in demand . . . . you must try to get as much mileage out of each piece as possible . . . . you must make sure your dollar per hour rate is high, and that month after month you are pushing for more money and aiming for the money goal you want.

HOW TO MAKE YOURSELF A SPECIALIST
IN A PARTICULAR FIELD

Again, this is not very hard—but it will require a little discipline. In the first place, pick out a field which you like, and which you seem to have a feeling for. Then go through the popular magazines readily available and start reading every article on this subject. Also, go to the library and look up these articles in the *Reader's Guide to Periodical Literature*.

In addition, make a list of the books in this field and systematically start acquiring them for your library.

Start reading technical journals—if it's medicine you're interested in, take the *AMA Journal* and others. In the beginning, look at only a few articles. Many will be a struggle to get through, but you'll find they do provide good research information.

Finally, make yourself aware of any indexes in this particular field. Your librarian can tell you about these.

After this, the rest is up to you. A writer doesn't have to know everything he's writing about, but he must go to somebody who does. On your first article, try to find somebody in your area who's an authority on your subject. Then try to establish who the national authorities are and write to them, asking specific questions for quotes. When you're through, if you have any doubts, send your article to these national authorities for checking—for the major magazines, this will prove to the editor that your article is really authentic.

Basically, however, you must continue to work in the field, continue to build your own files, collect voluminous literature on the subject, and read extensively.

THREE WAYS TO CASH IN ON A PARTICULAR SPECIALTY

1. *Try a short newsletter:* Specialists find editors often come to them in search of new ideas because they're more aware of developments in a particular field and often know the field as well as the experts.

One specialist takes advantage of this with a monthly newsletter which simply sketches the significant news developments in the field. This, of course, helps keep editors abreast. Many editors, this specialist finds, often pick up the phone and ask him to do something that is mentioned in his newsletter. You can do the same.

2. *Send tear sheets to people you've done articles on:* Also, drop copies to the local newspapers—the more publicity you get on your specialty, the more often you'll get local assignments. One free-lancer found, after doing this awhile, that he was being offered lucrative public relations assignments by local groups. In addition, he found himself in demand locally as a speaker, for which he could charge additional fees.

3. *Send tear sheets to all possible reprint markets:* Reprints in noncompeting fields can add considerable extra income. In one case, an article I did for *Outdoors Magazine* was picked up by *Sea and Pacific Motorboat* and later for several other magazines, for a total take of almost $600.

The problem is not enough editors are aware of your article. One specialist solves this by deciding on all possible fields that might take his piece, he then has 100 copies made up by a quick-print service and sends out to every possible magazine that might be interested—the results are many additional sales.

Checking on Chapter 7

Specialization does pay. By specializing you can write more in less time since you can double up on your research—do it more efficiently—and know where the sources are without having to look around.

Magazines buy more readily from an expert and pay more money. This is especially true if you make a name for yourself.

Becoming a money writer in a specialty field means learning which fields are in demand. Utilize the basic principles of establishing yourself, publicizing yourself, and making every article really pay. It also means getting as much mileage out of everything you write as possible.

To start becoming a specialist, pick a field, read as much in your area as possible, start building your own personal library, read the journals in the field, learn who the specialists in the field are, and build your own files extensively.

To get more mileage from your specialty, try: (1) Using a newsletter; (2) Sending tear sheets to your interviewees and local newspapers; (3) Have reprints made and send to all possible reprint markets.

CHAPTER 8

How to Determine if a Project Is Worth Your Time

One of a writer's greatest faults is that he *is* a writer and not a businessman. Frequently, he can complete what seems to be a well-paying piece of work, and not make any money at all. Not only must you be well paid for a piece, but you must also be able to complete it in a reasonable length of time if you're to make big money.

Again, let me emphasize here that making big money doesn't necessarily mean getting paid $4000 for a single article (although it can). It means having as many assignments as you can handle . . . . and bringing your dollar-per-hour rate high enough for each hour of work so you can make $10,000 a year—or whatever you decide. You can do this with $1000 articles, $200 articles, $70 articles, or even $20 ones. The important thing is to make them all add up at the end of the year to really big money. The reason this book continually talks about $70 or $100 articles is that these are the easiest assignments to get . . . and there are lots and lots of them around. Despite the fact that these amounts themselves are fairly small, by following the techniques laid down in this book, you can easily make your yearly income really add up. So even if you never in your life hit *Reader's Digest*, or even make over $100 per article, you can still make big money free-lance writing.

Now, if you haven't sold your first article yet, you're going to ask yourself here, "Just what's he talking about?" After all, at this point, what you want most is to break into print and to heck with whether or not you make anything on it.

I agree, if that's the stage you're in—your first job is to sell; however, as we've proved time and time again in classes, that's actually the easiest thing in the world—practically anyone can do it. This is just a matter of following the simple rules we laid out in the beginning, and keeping at it until someone says, "Sold."

After that, there are two ways to look at writing. It's either a part-time occupation in which you want to make some extra money or a full-time one.

No matter which way you go, you'll want each and every project to bring maximum returns. After all, you only have so much time . . . . and, depending on how you manage it, it can either pay you well or poorly.

In the writing field today, it's awfully easy to get into the habit of taking every assignment that comes along, whether or not they're really worthwhile.

This chapter, then, is aimed at making every project really pay off, so your total income will really be big. To do this, you must make all your time and every project produce maximum income. Here's how.

MAKE A LIST OF THE VARIOUS PARTS OF A PROJECT

To tell whether or not a project is worth your time, you first have to decide what's going into the project. Let's take a typical trade journal article. Is it just a matter of sitting down and writing the article? Of course not. There are many different ingredients, each one takes time.

In your trade journal piece, we find, first of all, you've got to get the idea. This may consist of going through the newspaper searching for ideas, or driving around in the car looking at businesses, or nothing more than seeing something interesting when you're doing another interview.

You must also, of course, get in your car, go out, and actually do the interview. This may take an hour or two, or three or four—depending on how far away it is and how much information you need. When you get home, you're going to take a certain amount of time to organize the article, a certain amount of time to write it, and still more time to rewrite. Also, there's photography. If you do it yourself, you must develop the negatives and print the pictures. If you don't, you must take the film to a photo shop, go back to select the right 8 × 10's, and go back again to pick up the finished product. Finally, everything must be put together, captions written, and the article packaged. A list of the parts on this project would look something like this:

1. Getting the idea.

2. Interview and travel time.

3. Organizing time.

4. Writing time.

5. Revision.

6. Photography.

7. Photo caption writing.

8. Packaging and mailing.

Now let's look at an article I did some time ago for *American Home* (California edition). It involved, first, an interview with a local insurance company representative, an interview with a lawyer, review of material sent from a New York public relations firm, and a library search. Finally, it needed organizing, writing, rewriting, assembling, and packaging. Each article you do will have steps similar to these.

ASSIGN EACH PART A TIME QUOTA

This may be difficult at first but, with a little practice, it's possible to make an accurate guess of how long it's going to take. If you're going on an interview, it ordinarily won't take more than one to three hours, plus travel time. I live near Sacramento, California and when I go to San Francisco for an interview, I allow two hours for the interview and an hour and a half driving time each way for about five hours total.

Now let's take a look at a typical trade journal piece. First, it may not take more than ten minutes to dig up the idea, so let's estimate our thinking time at ten minutes. We then look at our interview time—say it took us five minutes to make the phone call asking for the appointment, 20 minutes to drive across town, another hour and a half to take pictures and talk to the storeowner, and 20 minutes to drive back. That's a total of two hours and 15 minutes. Let's figure it will take three hours to write the piece. (You'll have to determine your own writing speed as you go along.) Then let's say organizing took maybe 20 minutes (it was fairly easy to put together) and rewriting another two hours.

The total photography time we guess at three hours (by the time we get the pictures developed and dried). If we take it to a photo shop, let's guess at an hour total time. These figures when added together will give you an estimated time to do the article—an essential step in making the final decision of whether or not the article is worth your time.

ESTABLISH AN HOURLY RATE

About the only way you're going to be able to really tell if a project is worth the time and will help you get to a big-money income at the end of the year, is to decide what your time is worth. Are you worth $5 an hour? $10? $15? $20? In the early years, I decided if I could make $5 an hour, that was pretty good. Then, as I went along, I raised it to $10, and finally to $25. If you've sold a few pieces, I suggest you establish your hourly rate at between $7 and $10 an hour, then compare some of your projects and see if that's about what you're making per project.

COMPARE PROJECTS WITH EACH OTHER ON A TIME-DOLLAR BASIS

Once we list the parts of the project, assigning each a time quota, and establishing an hourly rate, we're ready to make some comparisons to see if the projects we've done in the past are worth our time and if future ones are going to be worth doing.

I have two writing jobs on my desk right now, so let's look at them and see what their value really is:

The first one has a $100 price tag. It's a series for *Trailer Life Magazine* on people who trailer full time. We got these in the first place by asking the magazine's readers to send us letters about their experiences full-time trailering.

Now I do these pieces by simply reading and selecting those I think will make good articles. I then make a list of further information I need and call the people. I literally interview them over the phone, asking for the information I don't have. Finally, I have them send me pictures. I put the material together, write up the article, and send it on its way.

The other assignment on my desk is a houseboat test in Oakland, about 70 miles away—$150. This means I have to drive down, spend six to ten hours on San Francisco Bay, and drive back.

Let's then list each part with its possible time requirements.

"Trailer Nomading"	Houseboating Field Test
1. Check-out time–20 minutes	1. Travel and work time–10 hours
2. Telephone interview–30 minutes	2. Organizing time–30 minutes
3. Organizing time–30 minutes	3. Writing time–3 hours
4. Writing time–2 hours	4. Rewrite–1 hour
5. Rewriting time–1 hour	5. Collating–1 hour
6. Collating, putting material together, and mailing–1 hour	
Total—5 hours $20 per hour	*Total*—16 hours $9.37 per hour

As you can see, the best-paying article (and the one that's going to help me make big money) actually brings a smaller overall fee. I should point out here that you have to watch your hourly rate closely. You can actually get quite good dollar rates for the project and still lose money because of the tremendous time drain.

HOW TO PRICE YOUR MATERIAL

In the beginning, you'll find it best to simply take what the magazine pays. Just send in your article without a price, and the editor will pay his going rates.

After you've done four or five articles for the same magazine, however, there's no need to accept minimum rates. You can get more. In addition, after you've worked in the same field for awhile, you should put a price on all work to insure that you won't receive an amount below what you can afford to work for.

To do this, look up the magazine's rates in the *Writer's Market,* then figure out about what your manuscript would be worth at listed rates. Maybe the magazine you're aiming for lists its minimum rate at $350. If this is what you want, simply send the manuscript in. If, however, you think the piece is worth more, or you need a large amount to meet your present "hourly rate," you are ordinarily safe in asking up to 35 per cent more than listed (if you have done a number of articles in that field and are a competent writer). Do this by putting: *Price $400* (or whatever you want) at the bottom of your query or in the upper right hand corner of your manuscript.

If your article is more complicated or contains more "real reader information" than the common, ordinary article in the magazine you're aiming for, you can probably go 50 per cent more and sometimes double.

In any event, I suggest that you ask what you think you have to have within the limits discussed above—and don't accept less.

Finally, of course, after you've arrived at what you think is a good price, by all means check it out by the methods we've suggested in this chapter and see if at this price it really is worth your time.

DON'T WORK FOR FUTURE RATE RAISES

Somewhere in your career, you're going to run into a magazine editor who says, "I'd like you to take this assignment—it doesn't pay too much, but we'll make it up to you later. As the magazine grows, we'll keep raising your rates."

It's a temptation. Here's an assignment that pays money —but at less than your standard rate. Good as they may sound, these promises seldom ever pay off.

Let me give you two examples: (1) a trade journal undergoing consolidation under a new publisher said although their rates were only $50 per article, they had plans for making the magazine grow and expected to increase rates soon. Three years later, the magazine's total advertising pages were about the same, their total income was slightly increased, and their rates were exactly the same. It just didn't pan out.

In another case, a publisher of several outdoor recreational magazines started a brand new one with the promise that the rates would be a little low, but he'd bring a particular writer along as things progressed. The magazine prospered. The advertising revenue doubled, doubled again, then doubled again. The number of articles carried almost tripled, but nothing was ever said again about raising the writer's rates. In the beginning, the editor took many articles from this writer. He received $1000 the first issue, $600 the next, $450 the next, then $150 —from there on it varied but never got back to $1000.

The fact remains that editors have good intentions but something often happens along the way. Either they change their direction or what they had in mind just doesn't work out.

You'll also find, of course, that an editor will give you about what you think you're worth. If you're apologetic and feel your articles aren't worth more than $50 apiece, then that's what you'll get. Some time try doubling or tripling that amount and see what happens.

I've done this several times thinking I'd be turned down and was surprised to find that my triple rates were accepted and sometimes even more was offered.

Over the years, I've come to the conclusion that you must set a price that's probably higher than you feel you should get, then don't do the article if the editor doesn't agree to that price. As your career goes along, you'll find you'll be able to get your price in most cases—and editors who won't give you good rates in the beginning probably never will.

While it's going to be tempting to do a piece in the hopes of getting more money in the future—it just never seems to work out.

EACH PROJECT MUST PAY ITS OWN WAY

Many editors expect one piece to pay expenses for another. And while it's often tempting to go along, you'll usually find the practice is a trap that will cost you money. Here's how it works. An editor will call and say, "When you're on a trip to, let's say Fresno, run into Joe's factory and pick up a piece on how he turns out widgets."

What the editor means is that he will pay for the actual interview and the writing, but he won't pay expenses or travel. He expects you to schedule four or five other articles to cover his costs. Again, it's a temptation to let him get away with this, but it isn't cricket.

Every editor who gives an assignment should expect to pay for the time and expense of the piece from your desk back to your desk: all writing time, all travel, meals, motels, telephone calls, and anything else that's necessary to get the article in the mail.

I call this practice of trying to get out of legitimate expenses "piggybacking" and find there are very few other businesses that will allow it.

In effect, these editors expect you and other editors to help pay their operating cost—to help produce their magazine.

This probably wouldn't be so bad if it didn't hurt the writer. But in practice, it never seems to work out. Many times I've gone to a city on the basis of two pieces at $100 each and found my afternoon's appointment cancelled. The arithmetic then works out something like this: maybe it takes two and a half hours to drive, four hours to interview, and another two and a half hours to drive back. In addition, since it's 150 miles from home base, you bought lunch. At 10 cents a mile, that's $30 for the round trip, $3 for lunch. Subtract $33 from $100 and you have $67 gross profit. Add three hours for writing, an hour for revision, an hour for photography, and a half hour for organization. Divide this 15 hours into $67. You find you're receiving just over $4 an hour—not very productive, is it?

Now, if we'd done two $100 pieces on this trip instead of the one, we'd come out somewhat better. $200 minus the $33 is $167. To our original 15 hours, add another four hours for interviewing on the second article, another three hours for writing, another hour for revision, and an extra hour for additional photography. Divide this 24 hours into $167 and you get a little over $7 an hour—still not very good but certainly far better.

HERE'S A HANDY GUIDE TO DETERMINE
THE VALUE OF EACH PROJECT

Costing each project is extremely easy. It's simply a matter of figuring everything on a straight per hour basis. Here's what you do: When you complete an article, figure out the time and expenses involved. Make sure this includes travel, meals, motels, telephones, even newspapers. When payment is made, deduct expenses and divide the remaining amount by the number of hours involved. The result is a rate per hour. Armed with this, you'll be able to determine just where you stand.

In figuring your time, be sure to add letter writing, preliminary negotiation time, organizing time, and anything else that can logically be assigned to that article.

Here is a form that will help you keep track:

Title: _____	Total hours: _____
Date: _____	Pay: _____
Price: _____	Rate per hour: _____

EXPENSES	TIME	TOTALS
.	.	
.	.	
.	.	
.	.	
.	.	
.	.	
.	.	
.	.	
.	.	
.	.	
.	.	
.	.	
.	.	

This will keep you aware of what you're doing and help you make sure all projects are worth your time. In addition, of course, it will give you a good bargaining tool. If you do a piece for an editor and it works out to $5.50 an hour because of unusual time problems involved, then the next time he calls, you can tell him, "I made $5.50 an hour on the last article and $10 an hour is the minimum I can accept. I need $150 instead of the $100 I got before." By keeping track like this, you can make sure you're on the way to making big money—and not just trading writing dollars.

Remember, making big money free-lance writing doesn't mean getting a large amount for each piece. It means getting your dollar-per-hour rate high for all your time and keeping it there.

Checking on Chapter 8

Making big money from writing means aiming directly at it. To do this, you must make sure all projects are worth your time.

You can tell if a particular project pays by costing it out on a dollar-per-hour basis.

The steps are:

1. *Make a list of the various parts of your project.* A number of things go into each article such as research, travel, etc. You should know what they are.

2. *Assign each part a time quota.* You will have to guess before the article is completed, afterwards you can tell exactly.

3. *Establish an hourly rate for yourself.* This is what you think you should be getting at this stage in your career.

4. *Work out a dollar-per-hour rate for each project.* To do this, put down what the project will bring. Sub-

tract all expenses, then divide the total time into the adjusted total price.

5. *Compare projects with each other on a time-dollar basis.* Sometimes the project that pays the most, either on a total-dollar or a word-rate basis isn't the most profitable. Each must be costed to make sure of what you're going to make.

Other points to remember are:

a. *Don't trade writing dollars.* Many writers change their type of writing constantly but the new projects they take on don't bring any more than the old ones. This means they're simply running in place.

b. *Don't work for future rate raises.* Editors will often try to get you to work for them at low rates now with promises of more money in the future. This seldom pays off.

c. *Each project must pay its own way.* Another editorial favorite is expense "piggybacking"; i.e., using your and other editor's money to subsidize expenses that should be charged to their article. In most cases, it should be understood that all expenses you incurred on their article will be charged to it.

CHAPTER 9

How to Sell Everything You Write

No matter how long you've been selling, you won't sell everything the first time out. I wish I could say that as soon as you become a really experienced writer, you'll sell every article. Sounds great, but it isn't true. No matter how you hedge your bets, you won't get 100 per cent return for what you put out, even if they're all on assignment.

A recent check on my own books shows that of the last 40 articles, 36 sold and four came back. Why?

Well, one was a column to a magazine that ceased publication. Even though it was assigned, the column came back and I wasn't paid. One had been held over a year by a magazine which finally decided they weren't going to use it after all. Why? Who really knows. Too much of the same type of material, they no longer had an interest in that particular topic, or maybe they decided just not to publish it. The third was a houseboat test. After we'd run the test, the manufacturer said, "My gosh,

I don't want that model publicized." By raising a fuss, I did get the editor to pay me half, but I still lost money.

As you go along you'll find there will be many reasons manuscripts don't sell. The editor changed his mind about the topic, they've done several articles in that area and don't want to do any more, the topic is no longer in vogue, there's an editorial change and the editor rejects all the previous editor's material, there's a shift in publishing emphasis, the magazine goes broke—a thousand reasons, and they're all valid—all reasons why you won't be able to sell everything the first time out.

In the beginning, of course, you won't sell everything because the editor doesn't think your material is up to par. But you'll soon get over that and be able to turn out material that is good writing technically. But still, no matter how perfect a manuscript you finally do, you'll never be able to come up to that 100 per cent mark.

YOUR WRITING MUST BE GOOD ENOUGH TO SELL

So far, in this book, we've been talking as if everything you write is good, solid magazine material. In the beginning, it won't be, of course, and you will have to do some work on writing techniques. The important basics I find are these: (1) beginnings; (2) organization; (3) theme or red line; (4) mechanics, anecdotes, statistics, quotes from authorities; (5) endings; and (6) revision.

While this is not a book on how to write, but one on how to make money from your writing, basically sound article writing is essential. These points will give you a list against which you can check your own work. If you're weak here, pick up a good book on writing fundamentals from this list or others, and correct your problems:

- *A Complete Guide to Writing and Selling Non-Fiction*
  By Hayes B. Jacobs–Writer's Digest, 1967.

- *How to Write for Money*
  By H. W. Gabriel–Prentice-Hall, Inc., 1965.

- *Writing and Selling Magazine Articles*
  By Omer Henry–The Writer Inc., 1962.

- *Writing the Modern Magazine Article*
  By Max Gunther—The Writer Inc., 1968.

- *Writing Articles That Sell*
  By Louise Boggess–Prentice-Hall, Inc., 1965.

- *Writing and Selling Feature Articles*
  By Helen M. Patterson–Prentice-Hall, Inc., 1956.

Here, however, are the article basics that will make your work acceptable or unacceptable from the very beginning:

(1) **Beginnings:** Beginnings ordinarily are from one to three paragraphs long and consist basically of two parts—a hook to catch the reader and a transition on into the body of the article (it also can include a curiosity arouser). Hooks usually take one of these eight forms (or combinations of them): (1) question, (2) striking statement, (3) direct address, (4) summary, (5) quotation, (6) statistical, (7) anecdotal, and (8) descriptive.

Here's an example of a typical question lead using the hook and transition correctly: (**hook**) *How often have you traveled and noticed colorful wild flowers by the side of the highway?* (**transition**) *If you're like us, you probably wish you knew more about those lovely flowers and shrubs* . . . . . . and we're off into the body of the article.

(2) **Organization:** This is probably the most important part of an article and is the reason why some articles seem hard to read, others clear and logical. I've never held to an "organizational article formula," but believe simply that all you have to do is arrange the parts in logical order. The procedure simply is to decide on five or six elements that belong in your article. For instance, in a business article we might say: "Why did the man go into business? . . . . How'd he start? . . . . How's he doing now? . . . . How does he drum up business? . . . . What are some of the details of the

operation?" . . . . then shift these items around until they logically proceed from one to the other. Points under each of these five or six main topics can also be handled in a similar manner. It's important here to make sure everything about the same subject is all together—you cannot have the part, for instance, about how our businessman got over a problem of a thieving partner in two places—if that happens, pull it out and put it together.

(3) *Red Line—Theme:* Ordinarily your title establishes the theme of your article. For instance: "How to Build a Table," "He Made a Fortune Moving Houses," etc. . . . . from then on, you must see everything in your article through the eyes of your theme—if you stray from the theme anywhere, cut it out. For instance, in the article on moving houses, you might run into some material on how your subject befriended three neighborhood children. Now you can't use the material unless you can see it through the eyes of your theme, so you might include it in your article in this way: "Although most businessmen don't have time for anything else on their way to acquiring a fortune, Mr. 'House Mover' is frequently involved in projects just to help people. For instance, on one job, he noticed three children standing on the corner watching every day and . . . . . ." Remember, you must stay with your theme at all times.

(4) *Anecdotes-Statistics, Quotes from Authorities:* An average article simply consists of five or six major points—the article on the man who made a fortune moving houses might include what a success he's made, how he got started, some of the more unusual jobs he's done, what the difficulties are, why he's so unusual as a house mover, and how this makes money for him. But you just can't tell your readers this—they insist on being shown and that's where anecdotes-statistics and quotes from authorities come in—they not only tell the reader, they prove it to him. For instance, under the heading why this man is so unusual as a house mover, you might mix up all three to prove your point. You can quote statistics showing he does ten times as many jobs every year as anyone else—have a statement

from the mayor saying, in effect . . . . he's the most unusual house mover we've ever seen and why—and give examples of three unusual jobs and how he handled all of them in an unorthodox manner.

(5) *Endings:* You may do two things basically with endings—tell the reader what you've already told him—that is, simply take the beginning, turn it around, and restate it in another way, or leave the reader with a thought, any thought . . . . "And as we left Lake Kitchigoomi we vowed that we'd be back again, and again, and again" . . . . that ends and leaves the reader satisfied—so does this . . . . "And as we left Kitchigoomi, we knew we never wanted to go back there again. Our three-year-old Kim summed it up like, 'What do I think of Lake Kitchigoomi Mommy? All I can say is phooey' "

(6) *Revision:* Four things here: always try to say it in the fewest number of words—use active verbs instead of inactive —use picture words when possible, and wind up most sentences with a bang. Unfortunately, since this is not a book on how to write, I cannot give you the details of revision here, but I strongly urge you to buy *A New Guide to Better Writing,* by Rudolph Flesch and A. H. Lass, and thoroughly go over the chapters on "How to Save Words," "How to Find the Right Word," and "How to Give It Punch." If you really learn these rules your writing will be tight.

Now here's a checklist to help make sure your finished manuscript is professional and ready to go. (See next page.)

TIME IS ON YOUR SIDE

As you gain experience in writing, you'll find time is really on your side. The manuscript that came back today is not dead —just temporarily out. For instance, suppose you have a manuscript on how to use credit properly—it's made the rounds and nobody wants it. Fine, put it away and wait . . . . five months later the Senate starts an investigation of why people go bank-

MANUSCRIPT CHECKLIST

Items to Check	Acceptable	Needs Improvement
Beginnings—Does the first paragraph hook the reader well and provide a good transition to the body of the article?		
Organization — Does the manuscript proceed logically from one point to the next? Does it have material on one subject all together or is it scattered through the article?		
Theme—Is the title theme carried throughout the article; i.e., does every paragraph have something to do with the theme?		
Anecdotes, statistics, quotes — Are they smooth and well done?		
Endings—Do they tell them what you told them? Or leave the reader with a thought?		
Revision—Is the manuscript tight? What about inactive verbs? Picture words? Does every sentence wind up with a bang?		
Other—		

rupt and there is a great cry over the improper use of credit
. . . . out comes your manuscript for almost a sure sale.

I play this game quite avidly in the trade journal market. For example, one week I shot six shorts in a discount store (pictures with captions on a good merchandising idea), sent them in, and the editor fired them back . . . . five months later, I got a letter from the same editor that he needed picture shorts badly and did I have any he could use . . . . the same six went back in and sold immediately.

Manuscripts, as we mentioned before in this chapter, get rejected because the editor is overstocked . . . . isn't interested in the material . . . . feels the material is not topical . . . . feels it doesn't fit with the magazine's present policy . . . . just doesn't have the money . . . . and more. All of this can and frequently does change however—and for this reason you often find what was not acceptable six months ago is now in demand. So never feel your material is dead, watch and wait, and if something changes, send it back.

Here are the changes to watch for:

1. *New developments:* Let's say you're doing an article on the dangers of atomic power plants and it's rejected (even though as far as you can see it's a good strong, well-developed article that really meets the needs of the magazine). You put it away —then it develops through several studies that atomic power plants in several locations are a real danger and the press starts to make a fuss. Pull your article out and send it on its rounds again—now that there's new public interest, it'll probably sell.

2. *Any upswing in public interest:* Any time the public (or specifically a magazine's public) begins to get interested in a subject, you can be sure the magazine itself will take another look. As an example: articles on consumer problems, such as gouging by certain kinds of finance companies, received only a lukewarm welcome at one time; but after the housewives grocery boycott, Ralph Nader's automotive crusade, and government interest in consumerism, there was a great demand for this type of article.

3. *Change in magazine emphasis:* Magazines frequently change emphasis and format. They often decide what they were stressing wasn't quite right and begin putting emphasis in other directions. At one time *Lawn/Garden/Outdoor Living* used to run many articles on garden center merchandising . . . . suddenly there was a complete editorial flip-flop, and they began running more pieces on servicing, equipment, technical plant articles, and similar pieces.

   In the same vein, *Cosmopolitan* magazine changed overnight and began running pieces primarily oriented to the single girl; when this happens, any articles you have along the lines of the magazine's new approach, should immediately be sent in.

4. *Letters to the editors:* Let's take an example: you have an article on gun control—the editor has turned it down—then a few months later you begin to notice a number of letters from the readers in favor of gun control. Do you leave the manuscript in the file? Of course not! If the readers are now starting to show an interest, the editor may be in the market for a more detailed report—so send it back again.

5. *Editorial changes:* This is practically the same thing as letters to the editor—except this time the editor senses the change and begins writing about it. Some time ago, I began a whole series on the importance of consumerism in retailing and what the businessman could do about it. The series went over well, but one magazine in particular turned down all my ideas. Then six months later I noticed the editor had devoted his entire editorial page to the importance of consumerism and how it affects business. I dug the idea out, sent it back in, and sold it promptly.

6. *Changes in thinking among leaders in a particular field or industry:* Again, any time emphasis shifts, you can probably sell articles that couldn't be sold before. A good example is heart transplants. Before Dr. Christiaan Barnard made the first one, you couldn't give these articles away. Afterwards, if you had a good direct approach, you had a market almost anywhere.

These aren't all the changes that will affect the salability of your writing—but they are the major ones that will enable you to tell when to do a particular topic, and also when to send manuscripts back in that have already made the rounds and just didn't make it.

EVERYTHING HAS A MARKET— HERE'S HOW TO FIND IT

Literally everything has a market, so never feel that what you write is unsalable just because it doesn't seem to fit the markets you know—the trick is to think in terms of readers, not markets. Ask yourself who would be interested in this material—what magazines will these readers read. Let's say you have an article on famous waterfalls . . . . who would be interested? . . . . children? . . . . sure . . . . so start querying the children's magazines . . . . what about women? . . . . this usually isn't a woman's topic . . . . what about general family audiences . . . . sure . . . . so start thinking of the Sunday newspaper magazines that are directed toward leisure . . . . what about travel magazines and others, of course.

Now here is an example of how a working writer does it. A noted business writer, Omer Henry, was doing an article on a successful furniture retailer for *Lamp Journal*. While there, he noticed an attractive display of casual furniture (this became a piece for *Casual Living*). Some magazines like success stories of dealers who have utilized methods that would help other furniture retailers . . . . this became another piece . . . . and in the delivery department he found a large fleet of attractive Ford trucks that became both an article in *Ford Truck Times* and a *Commercial Car Journal* piece—all by keeping the needs of the magazine in mind.

The first approach, then, is to decide what groups of readers want to read what you have and make a list of the magazines serving these readers. The second approach, of course, is to do it more formally by using the market technique suggested in Chapter 3.

SMALL CHANGES OFTEN MAKE MANUSCRIPTS SALABLE TO OTHER MARKET AREAS

There are a lot of markets where you can sell the manuscript with a few minor changes that slant into their audience. Let me give you an example . . . . I recently did an article on a professional landscape maintenance service for *Grounds Maintenance,* a magazine for professional grounds maintenance people. This was a profile on the man who started the service and how it operated. This particular article sold the first time out. However, after thinking it over, I realized it would also sell to *Contract Services,* a magazine for executives in the building maintenance business. By simply taking it out of the owner's point of view and telling how the service itself solved particular maintenance problems, I had a salable piece—not a big change, but one which made the article acceptable to an entirely different readership.

You can do this dozens of times. In one case I sold an article to *Trailer Life Magazine* on what to see and do in Michigan's State Parks—then *Trailer Life* purchased *Camper Coachman,* a magazine dedicated to camper travel, and decided to run the series there. The *Camper* editor sent the article back and asked that it be redone to reflect the slant of camper instead of trailer owners. I looked it over, changed two words (trailer owners to camper owners), put "Camper Travel" in the title, and it went back perfectly acceptable.

Larston Farrar, in his book, *How to Make $18,000 a Year Free-lance Writing,* says much the same thing: "I'll never forget an article I did for a farm magazine. I thought it was pretty good, but the editor returned it. Then one day a writer at my request was reading a few of my pieces for marketing ideas. I pick other writer's minds just as you're picking mine. He remarked, 'this is a terrific yarn for a business magazine.' I hadn't even considered that with a few changes it would make a perfect business article, although business writing is my specialty. Actually, I revised it and sold it for $250 the first time out."

You can make rejected manuscripts acceptable then by thinking of the other possible areas that might be interesting. An entire viewpoint can be shifted by changing a few words— or in some cases by shifting sentences or paragraphs.

Consider what your readers want to know about the subject and what theme is necessary to give them their money's worth.

Here are the basic places to make emphasis changes:

1. *The Theme:* This often means simply changing title emphasis, then making sure that the text adheres to this all the way through. Recently, for instance, a business writer wrote an article titled: "The Images a Nurseryman Reflects." All he needed to do to change the article for the motorcycle field was to change the title to: "The Images a Motorcycle Dealer Reflects" . . . . and make sure that every place he talked about nurserymen in the article, he now talked about motorcycle dealers.

2. *Readership:* This sounds simple, but you'll find many articles suitable for several readerships—all it takes is to pull out the name for one reader like we did above and add another. A good example of where this can be done is in the outdoor field. For instance, it's possible a travel article could be "fixed" for many fields by starting out with trailerists, changing the readers to camper owners, to campers, to motor homeowners, or others—all easy to do.

3. *Structural Changes to Emphasize Different Points of View:* This is probably the most complicated of all. It usually requires some shifting of the manuscript parts. When you're doing this, I find it simplest to get out the scissors, cut the manuscript into individual paragraphs, and shift them around until they emphasize what you want them to. A good example here is a piece I did for both *Skin Diver* and *Ford Truck Times* some time ago, "Skin Diving for Gold." They were basically

the same article; however, the *Ford Truck Times* piece started with an example in action using a pickup, explained the basics of the sport, then told how the Ford pickup was used. This was fine for *Ford Truck Times*, but not for *Skin Diver*—so, to make the changes, the opening example was changed to one with the diver underwater . . . . the references to the use of the pickup were pulled and replaced with a quote from the diver about skin diving and where to start looking. The best thing to do here is simply decide which pieces of your article don't fit the format of the magazine you now want to send it to . . . . pull these . . . . add anything needed to emphasize the new approach and put it back together.

YOU CAN OUTWAIT AN EDITOR—NEW EDITORS OFTEN BUY REJECTED MANUSCRIPTS

It took me a long time to realize that every time an editor changes, it's a whole new ball game at that magazine. I'll give you an example.

I did an article years ago for *American Bicyclist and Motorcyclist*. The editor promptly bought it. Then I sent him two more and didn't hear anything at all. Finally I got a note saying they were going to buy. Two years later, since I hadn't heard further, I wrote again—no reply—I sent another letter, still no reply. A year after that I got one of the manuscripts back saying he'd intended to run it, but the store had been sold (this was a nasty note).

I wrote back asking what he expected after four years, and got a very nice letter back from a new editor saying he'd make things right and did I have more. I immediately bundled up everything that had been rejected at this magazine in the past. The new editor bought it all and asked for more. Over the next six months, I sold him 16 additional pieces. Then editors changed again—this one bought the next two pieces, then wrote asking if I'd do six additional ones—three were published and three are still waiting—two years later. I'm not sure why this situation happens, but it does—I can only tell you that every time an editor changes, pull out your rejected manuscripts and anything else close to what he's using and send them in. Chances are you'll sell something.

KEEP UNSOLD MANUSCRIPTS IN MIND AT ALL TIMES

If you concentrate on marketing and making big money, you will constantly be learning of new magazines who are in the market for material. Therefore, you should always be thinking of your unsold manuscripts with the idea that sooner or later you're going to run into some magazine who will buy what you have on hand.

In my own experience, I did an article on a nursery which turned the main building into a "trim the tree" shop at Christmas. This was an interesting article for a business magazine. I sent it to a magazine in the field I was working for, in this case *Lawn/ Garden/Marketing,* and promptly got it back with a note saying the editor had too many manuscripts at this time. I re-sent it to *Home and Garden Supply Merchandiser* and got it back again with a note saying they'd like to buy one picture.

I put the manuscript away and forgot it—then several months later I received a copy of a trade journal I'd overlooked, *Southern Florist and Nurseryman.* I submitted a few things that were snapped up. Then I thought of my Christmas manuscript, dug it out, shipped it off, and made a prompt sale.

This will happen dozens of times as you go along. A student of mine did an article on model trains which was rejected by the local newspaper. One night in class I brought in a retirement magazine, *Retirement Living,* she looked through their hobby articles then suddenly said, "I'll bet with a few changes, they'll buy my manuscript." The result was a prompt sale.

So, learn to think back over your rejected manuscripts as you come to new markets and ask yourself, could this be made to fit?

Checking on Chapter 9

You can sell everything with good marketing techniques. You, however, will never sell everything the first time out . . . . but you can over the long haul by keeping at it.

Your writing must be good enough to sell. Work on improving your beginnings and endings, the organization, the theme, the mechanics, anecdotes-statistics, quotes from authorities, and revision—the checklist in this chapter will help.

Time is on your side. If there are new developments in the subject you're writing about, there's a shift in public interest, change in magazine emphasis, strong upsurge in reader interest, shift in editorial thinking, or shift in thinking among leaders in the field you're writing on, start sending your manuscript out again.

Everything has a market. To find it, ask yourself what groups of readers will be interested in this subject? What magazines do they read? You can also systematically use the market search system in Chapter 3.

Small changes may make a manuscript acceptable to other market areas. After you've finished a manuscript for one field, try to decide if, with a few changes, it might be acceptable to another. "How to Cook a He-Man Meal" might be a piece for some men's magazines. With a few shifts of emphasis, it might also make a good one for the women's magazines. Basic places to make changes are with the theme, the readership emphasis, and the article structure.

New editors often buy rejected manuscripts. For some reason, new editors often take material that the old editor has rejected. This may be because the material is fresh to him or he wants to stress different areas. Whatever the reasons, every time the editor changes, pull out any material you think might be close to what he's looking for and send it in.

Keep unsold manuscripts in mind when looking over new markets. Every time you pick up a magazine, ask yourself . . . . do I have anything finished they might be interested in?

CHAPTER 10

How to Use the Interest
of Your Writing—Not
the Principal

After you've been writing articles awhile, it's a great temptation to think in terms of numbers. An article brings maybe $20, $100, $300, $4000, or more. To increase your income and make big money, most writers feel you must sell another. This is true, of course, as far as it goes, but every time you sell one article, then start fresh and sell another, it means you have to begin new. You get no extra income from what you've done and you certainly don't build, so your income increases without additional work.

That's fine if you don't mind limiting your income, but if you're trying to make big money from your writing as we are, then both your time and money must multiply itself.

Here are some ways to make each piece of work pay several times over.

BUILD YOUR INFORMATION FILES
WITH EVERY ARTICLE

A lot of writers use their files simply to store sold articles, but I use mine to store information as well and I suggest that you do the same.

In the first place, I went through and set up my article files by 102 topic headings, under such subjects as *sports, children's wear, motels,* etc. Every article I do in those particular fields is filed with all the information I accumulate on the subject. Over the years, then, I find if I'm working in a field and need additional information, I can go to my files and pull pieces of my own articles to make other articles.

For instance, as Field Editor of *Family Houseboating Magazine,* I do many houseboat tests. As a result, I have a huge file of houseboat test articles, plus a lot of additional information. Now suppose I decide to do a houseboat roundup and need to know a little about each one—all I've got to do is pull my own file and there it is, complete detailed information.

HERE'S HOW TO GET MORE SALES MILEAGE
OUT OF A FINISHED ARTICLE

When you finish an article, never put it away and say that's that. Put it on your desk and say, "All right, I've done the article. Now what other sales can I get out of this particular information?"

Let's say that you did an article on a particular lake for an outdoor magazine—in the process you shot pictures of the resort and people camping. You also came up with much additional information. Do you think others within driving range might be interested in a trip there? If so, this lake might well make a subject for the Sunday section of a nearby metropolitan newspaper. Think also about other market areas—what about trailer magazines? I don't know any that will take articles on a lake, but maybe they would if you wrote up the surrounding area as well.

Also, what about doing that lake as a fishing story?—you've got some pictures—perhaps you can get others. If you can find a little fishing information, and have fished there yourself, you can probably come up with a pretty good story. As you go about your workday, look at every magazine with the idea that you can turn subjects you're now working on in many directions and begin to build toward a big-money income.

TRY TO DECIDE HOW MANY WAYS
YOU CAN TURN A SUBJECT

Here are some tips that will help:

Tip 1: Do It by Audiences.

For instance, when you're doing a personality piece, try to decide what business the man is in, what church he goes to, and what clubs and organizations he belongs to.

Suppose he's a Kiwanian—then you'll send off a query to the *Kiwanis Magazine*. Suppose he's outstanding and a former Boy Scout—try *Boy's Life*. Suppose this man is very unusual —has dedicated his life to helping people, is also a Presbyterian —automatically a bell should go off and you should try *A.D.* (a magazine combining *Presbyterian Life* and *United Church Herald*). The same is true of any other religious group or other organization (such as the Elks) he might belong to.

Tip 2: Try Tapping the Entire Subject Range.

Again, let's suppose you're interviewing an outstanding personality and find he houseboats, skin dives, trailers, and also owns a dune buggy. That means that you have an article for each one of those magazines—provided, of course, you get some pictures of the man doing each of these particular sports. Simply build your material around what and how he does it.

Tip 3: Think in Terms of Manufacturer Interest.

Whenever you're doing a story, consider the equipment. Suppose we're doing the tree farm piece again, and instead of single pictures, we query the International Harvester magazines to see if they'll be interested in a full piece on the subject. We also query *Ford Truck Times* to see if they'd like a tree farm piece using Ford equipment—both are good possibilities. Practically every manufacturer has at least one house organ, and many have more. By looking them up in *Gebbie House Magazine Directory* and querying, you can often get several articles out of the same material instead of one.

TIP 4: Think in Terms of Fields.

One of the ways to get more big-money mileage out of an article is to sell it in various fields. Now suppose you take a trip, let's suppose you drive up one side of Oregon and down another. Instead of thinking of the possibility of sales to *Travel Magazine,* let's think of what groups of readers and fields would be interested—the trailer field, the camper field, the camping field, some of the auto club magazines, and more. Of course, instead of traveling in a car for trailer magazines, you'd be traveling in a trailer or a camper (with pictures to match) for camper magazines, etc.—but this is simply just a matter of taking a literary license, and also taking pictures of campers, trailers, motor homes, and whatever you're going to need.

TIP 5: Get More Mileage from Other Age Groups.

Besides subject matter and field of interest, there are also common topics that are of interest to different age groups. For instance, some time ago I did an article for *Ford Truck Times* on "Skin Diving for Gold." I remembered at the time to pick up my additional sales with *Skin Diver, Camper Coachman,* and *Trailer Life,* but I forgot that other age groups would be interested and was extremely surprised when it was reprinted in *My Weekly Reader.* Something I should have considered myself.

So think in terms of age groups. There are currently four magazines in the retirement field—*Dynamic Maturity, Retirement Living, Mature Years,* and *Modern Maturity*—all take articles on activities for retirees.

Then there is the general teen-age market including *Boy's Life, American Girl, Teen Magazine* and others—plus the religious group consisting of upper teens, middle teens, the eight to 12 age group, and younger.

In some cases you can sell all of these. I can remember some time ago when one of my students did a piece on a visit to an observatory—this particular piece sold to a retirement magazine, to a general interest magazine under the title, "What You Can Learn at Your Observatory," and to several children's magazines in the eight to 12 year group on the theme "visit to an observatory." Five sales because the author remembered that it isn't necessary to stop at one age group. So when you have an article, ask yourself if either older or younger people would be interested, then write the versions of your article for these markets and send them off. This is the way to really build a good income while conserving your time.

KEEP WORKING YOUR ACTIVE SUBJECT FILES
TO FIND MORE WAYS TO USE YOUR MATERIAL

Once you've sold an article, don't quit looking for ways to sell it, for here's where you'll make big money. As you find spare time, go back and look through your files, thinking of the other market possibilities. Now take the previously mentioned five tips and apply them to each one of the articles in your files. Will that article on a man who keeps tarantulas as pets you did for the magazine section of the local newspaper be of interest to children?—then you should write it for those magazines. What about other fields? Properly handled, magazines in the popular science field and scientific digest might well be interested in this topic—so go again.

In practice, what I do is this: Every one of my articles requires pictures. Proofs are made of each roll and these are filed in large notebooks. When I'm searching for ways to use the files, I simply sit down with the pictures and start going through thinking of ideas. In one case, I had done a business article on a nursery in Oregon, which, in different versions, sold several times. I sat down one day with the files and noticed that the outside of that particular nursery was loaded with displays. Using those pictures, I did an entire 1500-word article on how this nursery used displays effectively. Result—another $70 sale; just because I kept going over my subject files, continually trying to find different ways to turn this material.

NEVER START NEW WITH AN ARTICLE PROJECT

Always build from something you've already done. Every time you start an article project in a field or an area you've never worked in before, it means you must start from scratch to build up your background material and this keeps you from reaching your money goal quickly. If you've done a number of articles in a field, these articles provide research material to fall back on. You also have certain background information in your own mind that's helpful. You should, if possible, always use this material. I had one student writer who retired from the Fish and Game Department and kept all his articles in this field.

First he did an article on abalone poaching, based on his own experiences as a Game Warden, then he did a humorous article for *Sports Afield* on all the silly excuses game violators used—again, all the research was done. After that he did a hunting article on snipe—again, right in the middle of his field and something he had already done. He also did an article on Bryce Canyon—an area he had visited in his travels.

So when you are considering doing articles, try to keep in mind what you've already done. Think of what you've seen on the trips you've taken, some of the things you've done, and other article possibilities which will use at least a portion of your material without extra research.

TRY TO WORK IN RELATED FIELDS SO ONE
ARTICLE ALWAYS MEANS TWO OR THREE MORE

There are fields that overlap so thoroughly that when you do an article in one, you almost automatically come up with one in another field—and multiply your income quickly.

A good example of this could be trailers, campers, motor homes, the outdoors, and camping. An article called, "The Indians Invite You to Their Reservation" could be turned for several of these.

In building my writing business, I try to keep my fields all related and tied together. For instance, I like to work in the drug field, the toy field (to an extent), the sporting goods field, the grocery field, the rental field, luggage and leather goods, the automotive field, and others which more or less overlap. Now how does this work?

Well, a good example is a home and auto store with a good rental ski program and a top-notch ski department. This sold to an automotive magazine on how one of the chains merchandised skis, to a sporting goods magazine on the entire program, and to a rental magazine on how to effectively rent skis. All because I was working already in fields that tied together.

If, however, you work everywhere at once, you'll have trouble—say you do an outdoor article, then a religious article, and next an article on materials handling—nothing will tie together and you'll have to start new with every piece to build toward your big income goal. This, of course, is spinning wheels.

THE ONLY EXCUSE FOR STARTING NEW IS WHEN YOU'RE TRYING TO WORK INTO A NEW FIELD

Let's say you're working in the outdoor field on trailer articles, camping articles, and others. You feel that boating would add to your writing income and give you extra articles in all fields. This, then, would be an excellent reason for trying to break into the boating field. You'll find, however, you're going to have to put in a lot of extra work to become acquainted with what's going on. You'll have to do one article, then another, until you finally build yourself a solid information base. When you do, however, you'll have a field that will work in with all others.

In general, however, you should not take on a new field

or a new area unless it ties in with what you are already doing —otherwise, you will be using the principal of your writing and not the interest. But if the field ties together, then you will be able to take the article you just finished and build additional pieces in your other areas, plus, of course, beginning to multiply your income tremendously.

SPIN-OFFS ARE A VITAL PART OF YOUR INCOME

When I say spin-offs, I mean anything from an article that can be sold to another magazine, from a filler, to a couple of the pictures. Usually you have to keep this in mind when you're doing the article. This works especially well in the trade journal field, but can be done in other fields too.

Suppose, for instance, you do an article on "Logging with a Helicopter." Here's what we find: they're using some caterpillar equipment, have one or two Ford trucks sitting around, and other pieces of equipment.

Your mind should immediately jump to the spin-off possibilities. Get the caterpillar equipment in action—do the same with the Ford trucks and all others.

Now go through a copy of *Gebbie House Magazine Directory* (you'll find this in the library). Find out what magazines are put out by International Harvester and send these pictures to them. Do the same thing with Ford. If you want to, you can probably turn the Ford piece into a regular article for *Ford Truck Times*—but I'm talking about selling short pieces rather than articles. These are easy to do, yet bring additional money—sometimes as much as the article itself.

Roundup Articles and Books

You should always consider using your material as many times and as many ways as possible. The first thing to think of is the possibility of roundups.

This is simply a series of information collected from different areas on the same topic. Let's take the outdoor field, and say you've done 15 articles on traveling with a trailer up and down the West coast. All right, now let's take ten of the places you consider unusual and do a roundup called, "Ten Spots for Rec-V Travel on the West Coast." This simply takes material from every one of your articles and combines it into one. You can do this in practically every field.

Over the years, I have done a number of articles for trade magazines on the speed and custom business—these are the stores selling chrome wheels and that sort of thing. In practically every story I devoted a portion to the kind of advertising they did. Then I got an assignment to do two pieces on the most effective types of advertising speed and custom dealers use. Did I go back out and interview speed and custom dealers? No! I used the interest of my writing, went back through my own work, pulled out everything that pertained to advertising, and put it all together in a single article.

It's possible to make roundups of favorite recipes, the best ways to use credit, and much more.

I once had a student, for instance, who frequently referred to the habits of movie stars in his articles. To find this information in the first place, he simply wrote to their publicity agents. When he had done 20 or 30 articles, he pulled out all parts that referred to the stars' smoking habits and came up with an article on "How the Movie Stars Gave Up Smoking"—another example of using the interest of his article and not the principal.

Actually, there's no better way to build toward your money writing goal than to take your old work, and turn pieces of it into salable articles—or to take all of the work itself and turn it into books.

Here's an example of how I've done this in the past: In the first place, I, myself, did a number of trailering travel articles over the entire West. Several years later, I realized these would make a good book. I queried Trail-R-Club of America, who is probably the largest book publisher in the trailer field, and asked Bob Nulsen if he would be interested in a trailer travel book on the West, using those articles. He said "Yes"—so it was simply a matter of arranging them in order, doing a little bit of editing, and sending them in.

So keep in mind every time you're doing a series of articles that eventually you can turn these into books. If you think you've got a possibility, sit down and write the publisher, telling him what you've got and asking if he'd be interested in seeing a prospectus and a couple of sample chapters.

Actually, of course, it's good to keep in mind when you're interviewing people that you may do a roundup later. In fact, one writer I know has at least ten going at all times. A good example of these is our movie star roundup—how they gave up smoking. You could do hundreds of others—how famous people met their wives, how the famous rich live, the favorite diet of disc jockeys, and more. These are just roundup pieces.

Fillers (Short Paragraphs)

Another excellent field where you can really capitalize on what you've already done and add to your big-money income is the filler market. Today there are hundreds of fillers bought each month. These are simply jokes, recipes, anecdotes, or similar items used by editors to fill end of column or bottom of the page spaces. Readers often like these items so well they search them out first.

Fillers can actually be by-products of your regular writing if you gear yourself that way. You'll find them when you're interviewing, typing manuscripts, searching for material, and dozens of other ways. Suppose you're doing an article on child rearing; some of the items you don't use in the body of your articles may be sold for small checks . . . . maybe it's an article on how to give a child's party—some of the games may make useful fillers.

There are dozens of others. *Popular Mechanics* buys How-to-do-it short pieces on craft projects and shop work with photos and drawings. *Moody Monthly* uses newsbreaks and inspirational anecdotes. *United Methodists Today* buys church-related or family-related humor. *Parents Magazine* takes parental problem solving anecdotes for "Family Clinic". *Woman's Day* buys community projects and unusual activities for "What Goes On Here?" and also practical suggestions on homemaking and child-rearing. Many other magazines buy similar items.

The key to selling fillers is the same as it is for selling articles and other materials—you must know your markets.

Since each magazine has its own filler requirements, you must match these. The starting place is the *Writer's Market.* Filler requirements are listed here under each magazine. For a start, run through the publications in *Writer's Market,* looking over the items they take and their requirements. As you see the magazines themselves, read through the fillers and notice how they're constructed. One writer, using this system continually, keeps his eye open as he looks for material, does research, interviews, and writes. This material is then popped into filler folders marked "bright sayings," recipes, shop hints, etc., to be worked up for the magazines later.

Picture Shorts

If trade journal articles are your strong point, by all means don't overlook shorts as a supplemental income. If there's any way to use the interest on your writing instead of the principal, here it is.

Many times while out doing a $100 trade journal article, I've finished my interview, then looked around and added an additional $100 with "shorts."

These generally are merchandising or business principles written up in 50 to 100 words and illustrated with a picture (Figure 1).

Let me give you an example. While out doing articles with another writer one day, I noticed a houseboat parked in a shopping center lot with a big sign saying "Rent a Houseboat."

Figure 1. Themed Windows Sell Merchandise.

Customers always identify better with merchandise displays when they are tied to something they can thoroughly understand.

This one used in the window of Congdon and Crome, Palo Alto, California, needs no further explanation.

Typewriters displayed here are geared to student needs and several prices are shown to offer variety.

Back to school is stressed and the idea planted that a typewriter can help students get better grades. Charge card plaque is used to indicate that all merchandise can be charged and purchased easily.

We stopped and took a picture—across the street was an unusual equipment rental sign—inside the rental operation I decided to do a story on some mannequins being used in the display (another picture)—also an unusual tool rack (another picture) and a slotted board to unscramble pigtail adaptors (another picture). Finally, across the street, as we were leaving, we spotted another sign at a rental yard calling attention to itself by giving baseball scores (still another picture)—put together with a short description, these sold to *Rent-All* for $10 a piece. In the final analysis, the story brought $80, the shorts $60—certainly worth paying attention to.

In doing business shorts, look for good displays, unusual signs, and easier ways of doing things. Primarily shorts are a pictorial representation of basic merchandising concepts—and any time you find a merchant doing these, you can be sure of a sale.

Here is a list of several "short" concepts I've come up with over the years:

1. *Aisle Interruption Breaks the Monotony:* Remember how boring long aisles are—anything that helps break this up is salable. For instance, in the middle of a long gondola of breakfast food, a store builds a huge vertical display of bowls —it ties in, yet the display breaks up the long aisle and helps focus customer attention.

2. *Best Spot for Kiddie Goods Is Where the Kids Are:* A simple merchandising principle—a merchant simply builds a display where that type of traffic is. For instance, a grocery store might put a display of notebooks, pencils, and similar items right across from the comic books where kids will browse.

3. *Decoration Pays Its Way:* A two-way use of merchandise—for instance, artificial flowers might be displayed to enhance the store's appearance. The store also, of course, can get double duty out of them by putting them on sale.

4. *Selling Is Just Like Turning Pages of a Book:* I've used this so often, I'm sick of it—these are merchandise displays where you can stand at one corner and turn the hinged

display to see both sides. An example of this might be six display panels of buttons hinged to a counter post.

5. *Greater Visual Impact Results in Greater Sales:* An old one but still good—anything you can do to make merchandise more visible usually results in increased volume. Good examples of this often bring trade journal checks—one might be a big floor-to-ceiling display of skateboards lit by a big green spotlight.

6. *It Pays to Dramatize:* Anything you can do to put a little drama in your merchandise helps sell it. Let's say a sporting goods store sets up a complete camping display—with all the trimmings—a picnic table, simulated fire, and mannequins sitting around . . . . like they're really out in the woods camping.

7. *Framing Attention Means More Dollars:* Putting some sort of a frame around merchandise to attract attention often means more volume to the retailer—it's also an idea that will usually sell to a trade journal.

Learning to sell shorts means following the same rules as for articles:

1. Continually watch for good ideas when you are doing other things.

2. Study trade magazines regularly so you know what shorts these magazines are buying.

3. Send the short itself to all possible markets. If you've taken a picture of a fishing tackle display, for instance, look up all sporting goods magazines in the *Writer's Market,* or *The Standard Rate and Data Guide* and send out to one market at a time until it sells. Also, think of the kind of store. If taken in a discount store, this short can go to *Discount Store News*—if a drugstore, to *Drug Topics,* or others, and so on.

Short mechanical requirements:

1. Take pictures of displays, windows, and items that offer ideas other retailers can use.

2. Make each picture into an 8 × 10 glossy. Good quality is important.

3. Write the idea up. Make it terse and to the point (50 to 100 words).

4. Put words and picture together—this is done by placing the text on the upper half of a sheet of 8 × 10 bond. Leave the bottom half blank so it can be folded back and Scotch-taped to the picture.

Extra Home Projects

This isn't exactly using the interest on your writing, but it's very close to it. It simply involves making money out of projects that you do around the house you wouldn't capitalize on otherwise.

Here are some examples: noiseproofing a room, building a pickup camper, *leveling* the ground with a giant rake you've made yourself, stirring paint with an old sewing machine, using a felt collar with an oil can to apply oil uniformly, making plastic planters, bookshelves, making hot-dish coasters, shaping salt and pepper shakers, utilizing a different setup for bending sheet metal at sharp angles—the how-to of practically any easier way of doing something around the house.

There are basically four magazines that take these— *Popular Mechanics, Popular Science, Mechanix Illustrated,* and *Science and Mechanics*—(the last, is the smallest market)— they'll take home projects and useful tips—*Family Handyman* and similar magazines will take home projects, and from time to time magazines like *Woman's Day, Family Circle,* and *American Home* also will (although these are rather specialized).

Household tips, like installing a hall light from a pen light and hooking it up to your transformer (this sold to *Popular Mechanics*), are illustrated by one picture and about 100 words.

On bigger home projects, such as remodeling a room, be sure to take as many pictures as you can of every step, showing the project in all stages. Then sit down and query the magazines as to whether they'd be interested in the project. When finished, put it together just as they do the ones in the magazines. In some cases, you'll need a detailed list of equipment, in others it's simpler. Again, a good rule is to write it like the magazine does—follow this rule and you can't miss.

Checking on Chapter 10

Writers should continually try to use the interest of their writing not just the principal if they intend to make a big-money income—here are the ways to do it.

1. *Use information from one article to make others.* It's just good sense to try to use your information in as many directions as possible. Information about hotel travel rates in a travel article, for instance, might later be used in an article "Ten Hotel Travel Vacations You'll Really Enjoy."

2. *Turn your subject matter in as many ways as possible.* Keep asking yourself what magazines will be interested in this subject—direction—here are some tips:

3. *Tips:*
   (1) Decide how many different audiences (businessmen, religious groups, etc.) are interested in your subject.
   (2) Decide what areas of interest want your subject (skin divers, houseboaters, etc.).
   (3) Decide if some manufacturer will be interested. If your article involves a manufacturer's product, he may be interested for his house organ.
   (4) Decide which magazine fields will be interested (outdoors, sports, etc.).
   (5) Decide if your subject will interest different age groups, children, teen-agers, retirees, etc.

4. *Keep going back through your sold articles to find ways to resell that material.* Look at your articles and ask yourself will other magazines be interested in all or a portion of this, what magazines?

5. *Try to build on what you've already done.* It's a lot easier to do the second article than the first . . . . after that, your information builds progressively. Maybe there's a report in the files you can use, or a quote from some authority you picked up some time ago, and more.

6. *Try to work in related fields when possible.* Boating and skin diving, for instance, go together . . . . an article for one field may well yield a similar article for another.

7. *Start new only when you absolutely have to.* It's a temptation to keep working all over the map, but every brand new project means an awful lot of extra groundwork.

8. *Get extra mileage these ways:*

   a. *Roundups or books—Try to put the same types of information from a group of articles together to form one roundup article or a book.* "Travel in Mexico," *for instance, might be a book made up of a series of articles you've already done. You can also often ask questions for roundup articles when you're out interviewing for others.*

   b. *Home projects—Building a room? A fireplace? A different kind of chair? By all means take plenty of pictures, write up simple instructions and submit them to all possible markets.*

   c. *Fillers—Lots of times you come on filler material while you're doing other projects . . . . an old-time recipe, a humorous story, even something you'd* like to see them invent, can be sold. By all means, keep folders on these so they can be sent in later.

d. *Shorts*—Trade journal shorts are readily salable and can be done almost anytime. Carry your camera, take pictures of anything about business that strikes you—write up a short report and send it out to all possible markets.

CHAPTER 11

How to Turn Out Writing in Volume

No matter how you go about it, making money free-lance writing means turning out writing in volume. Twenty $1000 articles a year is $20,000. To make the same thing with $100 articles, you have to average about 20 articles a month. Can it be done? You bet it can!

Not right away of course. Twenty $100 articles a month, twenty $1000 ones, or a combination in between, producing $20,000 requires much shortcutting, much effort, and a great deal of know-how. In short, you must get maximum production from your time. Make no mistake, however, it can be done, for I have students who have achieved this level after several years of working in the field.

WRITING PRODUCTION MEANS
GOOD SCHEDULING

In the beginning you'll probably feel you don't need a schedule, but as you begin to turn out writing in volume, you'll suddenly realize time is vital. Many writers, in effect, fritter time away. Many who do two articles a day could do six, if they used their time wisely. You'll find, then, that in order to get the most out of your time, you're going to have to learn to use it effectively—you'll also have to learn to eliminate those activities which have nothing at all to do with production.

I know writers who sit and stare at the wall for an hour before starting to work. Maybe they're organizing and maybe they need this, but if they're just daydreaming, they should schedule that out. It's easy to fritter time away. You'll find in interviewing you can get interested and spend four hours instead of two—this is all right, once in awhile, if you both are enjoying something and want to pursue it, but most people will take your time if you let them.

The only way to use your time efficiently is to organize or schedule it. Larston Farrar, for instance, made a list each Sunday night of the things he had to do the following week. Then each evening he made a daily list for the next day.

A production writer's weekly list might look something like this:

1. Do piece for *Mobile Home Merchandiser*.

2. Write column for *Southern Florist*.

3. Do interview article on Senator Jones.

4. Write a query to the *Kiwanian*.

5. Do piece for *Specialty Salesman and Business Opportunities Magazine*.

6. Do interview for sporting goods piece.

7. Do research on camping roundup.

8. Write *Guns* material.

9. Write *Trailer Life* about caravan clipping.

10. Query *Camping Guide*.

11. Do photography.

12. Catch up on correspondence.

13. Write three chapters in book.

Each day he takes the items he wants to do and makes a daily list. By knowing what he is going to do next and continuing on until he's through, this writer saves a lot of time and continues making progress. This is a good idea that does work. I find I personally need more than this, however, so consequently I have devised some more complicated schedules that we will get to later in this chapter.

SCHEDULE EVERYTHING IN

The trouble with schedules is that sometimes you forget the little details.

For instance, at one time I found that I was answering the majority of mail, but letting a lot go simply because other things came first—I had several fights with editors over not answering some detail before I decided I had to reform. I also found that many times I'd come up ready to do an article, but hadn't taken time to request research material by mail, or I hadn't made the phone call I needed, or I was missing a photograph. Therefore, I decided the only real way to solve my problems was to schedule everything in.

I then sat down and broke my operation into all its parts. I advise you to do this also. Look at what you're doing every day and try to give it a label—then catalog it. If something isn't essential, get rid of it, but make sure you don't leave out some necessary step.

My own operation then looks something like this:

1. Answering mail

2. Actual writing

3. Revising

4. Querying

5. Preparation

6. Interviewing or research

7. Photography

8. Market Study

9. Upgrading thinking time

Preparation: This I find essential, and here's how it works: I was supposed to do an article for *Motel/Motor Inn Journal* on "How to Merchandise with a Menu." To do this piece, I had to decide who to interview, who to write for additional information, who to telephone for extra fill-in material, what pictures to take, and what other things I'd need. This only takes ten or 25 minutes. Preparation, however, assures you that you'll have all the information available when you need it.

Upgrading Time: I also consider this very important. You can work and work and work and never progress. One writer I know has made $15,000 for the last ten years. He does quite a few articles for such magazines as *Popular Science, Popular Mechanics,* and others. At this point, he knows from month to month that he'll be doing the same type of piece next month, and the next, and the next. This is fine, but you'll find that once you get in a rut like this, it's hard to get out. You have to work so hard to stay in place, that there's no time to progress. In this particular case, the writer decided that if he didn't do something he'd still be making the same income in another ten years. So he started adding books in his specialty by taking an hour each day out of his schedule. Other writers spend this time trying to figure out how to sell their articles other ways, how to sell the same article to industry, or how to up overall income.

One I know even devotes his upgrading time to trying to sell his writing services to business and in building up a consulting firm for companies who want to teach their executives to write better.

Every writer needs this kind of time even from the very beginning. He should schedule the time to sit down and see what he can do to make more money per article, what he can do to publicize himself a bit more, what he can do to enlarge his fields, and what other kinds of projects he can do that will make more money—this time, I believe, pays off handsomely.

Market Study: The same is true of this. The only way you'll ever hit magazines consistently is to spend time studying what they're doing, the directions they're going, and how they put their material together. Even if you're selling regularly, the only intelligent way to come up with articles for a magazine over the next year is to sit down and study what they've done over the last, and then try to decide what they might want to do next year—this is essential if you are going to keep progressing and have plenty of assignments. So always schedule it in.

YOU MUST WORK YOUR OWN WAY

In drawing up your own schedule, you're going to have to take into account your own operation and the way you want to do it. You'll also have to take into account your temperament —some people write best in the afternoon, others at night, others work better from six in the evening till one o'clock in the morning.

As I said somewhere else in this book, I decided years ago, after working for the larger magazines, that I really did best in the trade fields, in the outdoor fields, and others where I could do one interview and write one article.

Therefore, I set up my own schedule to take this into account. Now I find I'm actually pretty conventional from the work standpoint. I like to start about nine, work till noon, knock off till one-thirty, then work again till about six. I also try to do all actual writing on Monday and Tuesday. Wednesday afternoons I reserve for photography, and Thursdays for interviewing.

Usually I try to schedule three interviews every Thursday. Sometimes, however, for variety, I'll do the same thing all day. And about once every two months I jump in the car on Thursday morning and start driving in any direction I pick, working drugstores all day.

I find, however, that a writer must hang loose. I get some pretty "kooky" assignments now and then, and I must be able to handle them. For instance, I've been assigned to attend a houseboat wedding, do articles on how to assemble Mack Trucks, fly to Michigan to test houseboats, cover trailer rallies, do pieces with industry leaders, cover conventions, and a lot more. To do this, any schedule must be extremely flexible.

HERE'S ONE SCHEDULE THAT WORKS

Most of the time, however, I find I can establish a regular work week, confining my outside time to just Thursday. Now for scheduling purposes, I realize you cannot work straight through—at least I can't—so I divide my day into 40-minute periods and work 40 minutes, rest ten, work for another 40 minutes, rest ten, work another 40, rest ten, and every two periods I stop for 20 to 25 minutes and have coffee or something else. I time these periods with a mechanical timer that rings a bell at the end of the period.

CHART YOURSELF FOR A FEW DAYS

Are you using your time efficiently? Most writers aren't. But to see how you're actually utilizing your time, you should chart yourself for a few days, then correct what you're doing wrong. Simply keep track of yourself from the time you go to work in the morning until you decide to stop at night (See Figure 1).

In doing this, be completely honest and make sure you write down the time spent sharpening pencils, just idly reading, enjoying a talk on the phone, or anything else you might do.

At the end of the day, you may find your card looks something like this: 9:00 to 9:10, staring out window; 10:00 to 10:20, writing; 10:20 to 10:25, coffee; 10:25 to 10:40, writing; 10:40 to 10:45, drumming fingers on desk; 10:45 to 11:00, rearrang-

NEWCOMB SCHEDULE

PERIOD	TIME	MONDAY	TUESDAY	WEDNESDAY	THURSDAY	FRIDAY	SATURDAY
1	9-9:30	Mail	Mail	Mail	-------	Mail	Upgrade
2	9:40-10:20	Write	Write	Write or Books		Write or Books	
3	10:40-11:20	Write	Write	Write or Books		Write or Books	
4	11:30-12:10	Write	Write	Write or Books	I N	Write or Books	
Lunch	12:10-1:30				T	-------	
5	1:30-2:10	Revision	Revision	Revision	E		
6	2:20-3:00	Revision	Revision	Revision	R		
7	3:10-3:50	Query	Query		V	Query	
8	4:00-4:40	Prepare	Prepare	Photography	I	Prepare	
9	5:00-5:40	Market Study	Market Study	Photography	E W	Market Study	

Figure 1. My Writing Schedule.

ing pencils on desk; 11:00 to 11:30, talking on phone; 11:30 to 12:00, writing; 12:00 to 1:30, lunch; 1:30 to 2:00, writing query; 2:00 to 2:15, leaning back in chair; 2:15 to 2:30, reading a book; 2:40 to 2:45, rifling papers; 2:45 to 3:00, talking to friend who came in; 3:00 to 4:45, interviewing; 4:45 to 5:00, travel; 5:00 to 6:00, watering plants in yard; 6:00, quit work.

Now add up the time you have actually worked and the time you didn't do anything. Be sure and chart yourself for several days so you begin to get an accurate estimate.

Every day I add my total work periods and also make an end-of-the week total. Then I try to improve my performance. The column on the right includes all my common faults (see Figure 2). By making a note of how much time I indulge them every day, I can work at getting better.

Now in practice you're going to need some thinking time and time to unwind between jobs, so don't take all the slack out. But in an eight-hour day you should be able to get five productive hours out of yourself, and use the rest to smooth out the problems.

If you're not doing five hours of real work, then concentrate on eliminating those waste time spots by working through them.

I find, basically, if I can get six or seven productive periods out of every nine, that's pretty good. Try as I might, there is some slippage. In the first place, I have a lot of people calling to ask questions. It's always seemed funny to me that people would never dream of calling a businessman to ask a personal question in the middle of the day—but they think nothing of calling a writer . . . . and I've even had would-be writers call right in the middle of an article to ask if they could read poetry over the phone. These are the things you must eliminate if you're to get the most production for your time.

ASSIGN PRIORITIES

To make big money and turn out writing in volume, the one essential act is putting those manuscripts in the mail. Of

Daily Writing Success Chart

MAIL _____

BOOK _____

ARTICLE _____

ARTICLE _____

ARTICLE _____

REVISE _____

REVISE _____

REVISE _____

PREPARE-MARKET _____

DO IT NOW-MARKET _____

RESULTS: Useful time _____ Waste time _____ Articles written _____ Articles revised _____

SELF-IMPROVEMENT IS IMPORTANT

1. Talking to people _____
2. Waste time puttering _____
3. Going for mail too often _____
4. Coffee breaks too long _____
5. Leaving office too much _____
6. Doing other than planned activity _____
7. Time looking for material _____

Date _____ Time Started _____ Quit _____

Postives to Accentuate

1. _____

2. _____

3. _____

Negatives to Eliminate

1. _____

2. _____

3. _____

Figure 2. Here's a Form I Use That Works Well.

course, to do this you'll have to do research or interviewing; you'll have to do the actual writing and the other details absolutely necessary for turning out a manuscript.

In addition, however, every writer finds himself doing many other tasks. But in order to get maximum production, all tasks not directly related to actual writing, must be held in check.

For instance, in my own work it's nice if I send a thank you letter to everyone I interview—also a copy of the manuscript when the article comes out. It's also nice to return all calls and write letters back to everyone that writes me. Unfortunately, I find these things really eat into time and have nothing to do with production. In other words, I can eliminate them entirely and won't turn out one manuscript less a month.

As a practical matter, I answer every letter from editors. All others I put aside to be answered when I get extra time. As a result, once in awhile I really get bawled out for not answering my mail—but that particular piece wouldn't have brought me one extra dollar—and if it doesn't, then it must wait its turn.

In assigning priorities, then decide which tasks are essential and which are just so much fluff; take the essential ones and assign a priority number for the day or week and this is the order you'll work in.

MAKE UP MODELS OF ALL STANDARD LETTERS OR OTHER COMMUNICATIONS

One of the best ways to turn out writing in volume is to really cut down your letter writing. You can do this if you confine your original writing to longer letters and standardize the shorter ones. For instance, if you're in the habit of dropping a note to the editor with your article—why not make up one letter that will cover the general situation and mail it out each time. This will save a great deal of time. The one I use is simply, "Here is the trailer piece," or "Here is the piece on flowers," or whatever I happen to be doing, and just sign it. You should do this as often as possible. With queries, I have a mimeographed query form (Figure 3) with a checklist at the bottom. Since the editor can simply check and send back, I get replies much faster. The limited space also makes me hold the actual queries to two or three paragraphs. The entire form, of course, saves considerable time and work.

The same applies when writing an editor for money. No use making an original letter each time. Make a form and use it consistently. It's a real time-saver.

TAPE RECORDERS SPEED UP WRITING

Did you ever try to write longhand? If you did, you know what a difference it makes when you switch over to a typewriter. Similarly the time difference is just as amazing when you switch from a typewriter to a tape recorder. At one time, it used to take me three hours to type a standard 1200-word article. Now I can do the same 1200-word article in from 35 to 40 minutes on the tape recorder.

In order to give you some starting point, I'll detail my own procedure. In the first place, I own three Norelco Carry-Corders. These I purchased because they use cassettes instead of reels.

My typist keeps one recorder, I have a second, and the third is used to fill in, in case one of the others goes out. My work for the day is posted on a large bulletin board in order. I simply take the first piece down, pull the folder, and start dictating . . . . when finished, I go to the next. At this point in my career I can easily turn out four articles before noon, provided all the research and interviewing are done.

I then place the tapes in an envelope and put them in the mailbox. My typist picks these up after four in the afternoon and returns everything she's done from the previous day.

I take this typed material and place it in a box for revision. Actually I have my typist type everything in final form as

Mr. Howard Kelly, Editorial Director
Home & Auto Retailer
8 John Street
Southport, Connecticut 06490

Dear Howard:

SUGGESTED PIECE ON: <u>HOW TO REALLY MERCHANDISE BICYCLES</u>

Bicycles and their accessories, of course, form a pretty good market for
the home and auto retailer, yet many just don't do an adequate merchandising job.

This article will be essentially a roundup, showing the ways a number
of dealers have effectively merchandised bicycles, some of their ideas,
such as contests, having bicycles dropped from a helicopter with Santa
in it at Christmas time, and other stunts -- how they're effectively
displayed to produce more volume, the ways some retailers have merchandised accessories including tires and other items, and some of the bike
specialties they've gone into which help produce additional volume.
This will also include effective forms of advertising.

Let me know what you think.   Cordially,

                                               Duane
                                               Duane Newcomb
_____
Realizing that replying takes added effort, this brief query
and reply is being used to save your time.

Editor's comments:

_____Yes, go ahead with article. I need it by _____.

I cannot use now. Overstocked. Try again in _____ months.

_____No, it is not for us.

Specific angle or treatment desired other than mentioned in
query:

Figure 3

if I won't have to do any revision. This is the goal to be worked toward. In practice I find I still do a small amount which usually takes from 20 to 30 minutes extra an article. This then goes back to the typist the next day for retyping and finalizing. When it returns, it's put together with pictures and sent out.

In taping I put in all periods, all paragraphs, and all capitals. Difficult words and names are spelled out if I can. In the beginning I had a bit of difficulty switching from the typewriter to tape, but within a month I couldn't work any other way. The typist keeps track of how much she does, and so do I. Then once a month she's paid at the rate of 50 cents to 55 cents a typed page, plus additional amounts for different kinds of work.

To make my typist's job easier, I've also made up a complete model book which shows her how to set up a regular letter, how to set up a query, how to set up a manuscript, how to set up my columns, and how to set up the picture shorts. This way she doesn't have to ask me additional questions, she can just look it up.

TRAVEL TIME CAN BE USED FOR TAPING

I once used to tape all the time while driving, but I've practically stopped. There are, however, a lot of writers who still do most of their taping in the car. This is especially effective for trade journal pieces. When you come out of an interview, the facts are extremely fresh. When I tape, I start by simply sitting down in my car and working up a five-point organization on a card which I tack to the dashboard. Then I turn on my recorder and put the article on tape as I drive. By the time I get home after an hour's drive, I have my article done. This works quite effectively. The main problem I found is that if I need a date or other details, they're buried in my notes. I have no way of getting to them while driving. There is some objection that this is hazardous, but a lot of writers do it and I believe at this point, it's not illegal in any state.

WORK TOWARD TURNING OUT A
FINAL DRAFT THE FIRST TIME

Depending on which way you go, you will find it necessary, in some cases, to do final work in your first draft. This is especially true where you're working for the minor magazines for $100 an article or less. You just can't afford to take the time to revise if you expect to come out moneywise and keep your hourly rate high, Therefore, try to work toward a final draft the first time. This means good organization right from the beginning. What I do to make sure it comes out right is to jot down maybe six major points that are going in the article—then I move them around until they're in logical order, with a few details and points under each. After that I start to record, knowing I'll at least get the information down on paper in the right order. Basically, taping lets you come out with a clearer, more concise manuscript than you could any other way. But you will find as you go along that the way you talk is not necessarily the way you should write—you'll wind up with redundancies and will say things like "tiny little." You'll use incorrect tenses and make other mistakes. If you circle these on the copy and look them over carefully when you're through, you'll begin to get an idea of some of your common mistakes and can work toward avoiding them on tape.

DEVISE A SYSTEM

Probably the most important thing you'll ever do if you expect to turn out writing in volume and make big money is to use a system that's as foolproof as you can make it. If you don't, you'll find you're duplicating your effort in many cases.

Making big money free-lance writing basically means turning out writing in volume. If you go the higher money route, you must learn to cut down the time required on all details. If you go the specialty route, where your average article runs around $100, you have to learn to turn out from 25 to 40 articles each and every month.

First, I'll give you some standard pointers for doing more in less time, then I'll take you through my own system and show you how it works.

POINTERS FOR TURNING OUT MORE WORK

1. *Work Only on Productive Tasks:* Do those which lead to getting your manuscript in the mail.

2. *Assign Priorities to Your Work:* Do the steps that are most important first.

3. *Set Deadlines for Yourself:* This puts a pressure on you that is extremely helpful.

4. *Set Monthly Dollar Quotas:* You must pace yourself as you go along if you expect to make big money—if you decide on $50,000, start with what you can reach, say $600 a month . . . . then keep gradually increasing it.

5. *Prepare for What's Coming:* Make sure that you have all the information on hand when you're ready to write. Also, look forward to where you want to be in six months or a year, and see if there's anything you can do right now to get ready for this.

6. *Limit Outside Activities During Working Hours:* During prime working time, you can't do anything that isn't productive. It's awfully tempting to look up some information on a topic you're interested in, or read an interesting article . . . . but don't. Save that for after working hours.

Now let's look at my system briefly:

What I want to do, of course, is take every article from idea to finished manuscript as quickly as possible.

To do this, I place all incoming assignments on 2-inch tags and hang them on one of two 5′ × 3′ assignment calendars (current month, next month).

On the day I'm ready to write, the current day's work tag

is pulled off the board—the article taped—and sent on to the typist.

Ideas as I come to them (either from magazines or in the form of newspaper clippings or notes) are placed on a small 25″ × 30″ bulletin board. I also regularly query from the ideas on this board and study the markets.

Articles coming back from the typist are placed in the top tier of a seven-tiered horizontal file. Pictures as I complete them are placed in the second tier. When a manuscript is revised, it is placed in the bottom tier along with its pictures. The article is then ready to package and send off to a magazine. Since I send out 25 to 30 articles a month, what I usually do is wait until ten or 15 articles have piled up completed. I then package them all at once and send them on their way.

SPEED UP INFORMATION GATHERING

I can't really tell you how to do this, but when possible you should cut your research time to a minimum. This doesn't mean doing a sloppy job. It means combining steps and using methods to really concentrate your efforts. Here are a few ways: (1) Telephone instead of going out. Often you'll be tempted to jump in the car and drive somewhere for a short interview with someone whose information you need in your article. Don't! Call if possible, it'll save an awful lot of time.

(2) Combine library time when possible. Instead of going to the library to find material for one article, always be working on several at the same time, and gather what you need for all articles in one trip.

(3) Do a number of interviews the same day. There's a considerable amount of wasted time driving to one interview, then driving home. How much faster if you schedule three interviews the same day in the same section of town so you can go from one to the other rapidly.

As you go along, you should look for your own steps which allow you to speed up this process.

Checking on Chapter 11

Schedule your work. One easy way to make sure you handle everything is to make a weekly list of everything you should finish, then take a few each day. If you make a daily work schedule, however, you should break down your entire operation and make sure you include time for every step somewhere in your schedule.

Chart yourself. It's awfully easy to waste time. To try to plug these leaks, first you should try to chart what you do for four or five days down to five-minute intervals . . . . by all means list all negatives and try to eliminate them.

Do essentials first. It's awfully easy to waste time being extremely busy. That's no good, however, unless it actually results in turning out manuscripts. To insure this, assign task priorities and stay with them.

Standardize letters. Many letters a writer writes, including parts of queries, can be standardized. This way a letter-writing job of 20 minutes can be cut to less than one or two.

Tape recorders build speed. To really build speed in writing, a writer should try to use a tape recorder. Some writers find that they can cut time still further by taping in the car.

Cut down revision. Writers expecting to turn out volume, must cut revision time—this is done by organizing well beforehand, and by going over the revised manuscript, noting the mistakes you made, and working to correct them the next time through.

Systems are important. Unfortunately, not every writer can use the same system and yours must be tailored to your own working habits. By using calendar boards and flow production methods, however, you can speed up work.

Search for a system to speed up research and interviewing. Some of the ways are: (1) Use the telephone instead of making a trip. (2) Do library research for several articles at once. (3) Schedule a number of interviews in the same area the same day.

CHAPTER 12

How to Build Your Name
for Extra Profit

There's no doubt you can increase your income as you become more valuable to the editors. There are really two ways to do this. First build a reputation so editors know you'll turn out a sound piece of work on deadline. Second, build your name to a point where it is instantly recognized by magazine readers—to the point where they write about you to the editors, talk about you, and look forward to your articles every month. As far as I can see, you can do both jobs the same way. Anything you do to increase your recognition with a particular magazine's readers will also help build your reputation with other editors. The reverse isn't quite so true, but in this chapter we're going to concentrate on those things you can do to establish yourself with the largest possible audience and build a steady income. Now here are some ways to build your name.

TRY USING AUTHOR BLURBS

It's an axiom in this business that article writers are anonymous. For some reason, people pay little attention to a writer's name. To prove this point I often ask my classes who Frank J. Taylor is—out of several hundred, it's seldom I get one who knows, yet he has written for the *Saturday Evening Post* and the *Reader's Digest* for years and years.

In order to build your name then, you are going to have to do a little extra. The easiest thing you can do is include a blurb and a picture with each article (Figure 1).

This blurb should probably be not more than three paragraphs and directly related to the subject you are writing about —tells a little about you as a writer (and why you are qualified to write on this subject). This makes it interesting to the magazine's readers and more likely to be printed because it says you're an authority. The best thing to do is make yourself up a whole set of 8 × 10's and any time you do an article that's something a little extra, simply send along a picture and blurb. You'll be surprised how many times the editor will pick this up.

Along this same line, you can accomplish much the same thing by putting your credits on the back of your letterhead. Every letter you send out to an editor, then, lets him know exactly what you've done. Noted author Samm Sinclair Baker does this quite effectively (Figure 2) using not only a credit list, but his picture, his credits, and a brief bio.

PUT YOURSELF IN THE PICTURE

As you do a number of articles for the same magazine, one of the best ways to become identified by the readers is to put yourself in the article pictures. A tremendous example of this is Tom McCahill at *Mechanix Illustrated*. Pick up a copy of McCahill's articles, you'll see him there standing beside the automobile he's tested that month—this picture is usually large

About the Author . . .

A retired master of cruise and cargo ships for American President Lines, Captain Bill Magann isn't exactly a stranger to the high seas. After more than 25 years, in a career stretching from mess boy duty on a Great Lakes coal ship in 1929, to top command of around the world naval and commercial vessels, Captain Bill has really seen it all. His foregoing advice on open water houseboat cruising should prove salient text to the skipper heading out where its deep and blue — and where a good boat and accomplished seamanship are musts.

Figure 1. Author Blurbs.

Reprinted by permission of Family Houseboating Magazine.

and at the top of the article. Along in the article, you'll find another one or two of McCahill doing something else. With this impact, there's little doubt you're going to know who did the testing and wrote the article.

It isn't long before you begin to identify McCahill as a real

```
                                          July 14, 19__

     DUANE G. NEWCOMB

     Dear Duane:

        Nobody but nobody has the unfailing formula for success
     with a nonfiction book (even less with fiction).  Boiling
     it down, here are the steps I take in writing the books:

     1. Choose subject of interest to me.

     2. Make sure the subject is of interest to most people,

             of enough interest and importance so they'll pay out

             $5.95 or more for a book about it.

     3. Check with agent on possible publisher interest.

     4. Prepare an outline and first chapter.

     5. Write so that every page will provide specific and

             maximum help for the reader; make it readable, entertaining.

     6. Pray that the book clicks, meanwhile doing everything

             possible to promote it personally when it comes out-

             press, TV, radio interviews, etc.

        I've conducted workshops on THE NONFICTION BOOK, have
     stacks of notes, probably will one day write a book on
     the subject (although audience is very limited).

                              Best wishes,
```

Figure 2

Samm Sinclair Baker
1027 Constable Drive South
Mamaroneck, N. Y. 10543
Phone: (914) 698-5535

Biographical Notes

"America's Leading
Self-Help Author"
(N.Y. Times)

AUTHOR OF 23 BOOKS IN MANY FIELDS:

*5 BEST-SELLING DIET BOOKS with Dr. Irwin M. Stillman (over 15 million).
 *THE DOCTOR'S QUICK WEIGHT LOSS DIET (Prentice-Hall; Dell)...
  Best-Selling Diet Book of All Time -- over 10 million to date.
 *DR. STILLMAN'S 14-DAY SHAPE-UP PROGRAM (Delacorte; Dell 1975).
 *THE DOCTOR'S QUICK INCHES-OFF DIET (McKay; Dell).
 *THE DOCTOR'S QUICK WEIGHT LOSS DIET COOKBOOK (McKay; Bantam).
 *THE DOCTOR'S QUICK TEENAGE DIET (McKay; Warner Paperback Library).
*CONSCIOUS HAPPINESS (Grosset & Dunlap 1975; Bantam 1976).
*THE PERMISSIBLE LIE, The Inside Truth About Advertising (World; Beacon)...
  "First instance of such censorship in book publishing history."
*INTRODUCTION TO ART (collab. with wife, Natalie)..(Harry N. Abrams, Inc.).
*"DOCTOR, MAKE ME BEAUTIFUL!" w. Dr. James W. Smith (McKay; Bantam).
*YOUR KEY TO CREATIVE THINKING (Harper & Row; Bantam; Reader's Digest).
*1001 QUESTIONS & ANSWERS TO YOUR SKIN PROBLEMS (w. M.D.)(Harper&Row; Dell).
*HOW TO PROTECT YOURSELF TODAY (w. Police Official)(Stein&Day;PocketBooks).
*VIGOR FOR MEN OVER 30 (with MD)(Macmillan; Warner Paperback Library).
*HOW TO BE A SELF-STARTER (Doubleday)   *HOW TO BE AN OPTIMIST (Doubleday).
*2 MYSTERY NOVELS: *ONE TOUCH OF BLOOD   *MURDER, VERY DRY.
*5 GARDENING BOOKS (and Gardening Columns, Articles, Radio Series):
 *MIRACLE GARDENING ENCYCLOPEDIA (Grosset & Dunlap).
 *MIRACLE GARDENING (Bantam, a Gardening Best-Seller; many editions).
 *SAMM BAKER'S CLEAR & SIMPLE GARDENING HANDBOOK (Grosset; Bantam).
 *INDOOR & OUTDOOR GROW-IT BOOK for Children (Random House).
 *GARDENING DO'S & DON'TS (Funk & Wagnall's).
HUNDREDS OF FOREIGN LANGUAGE EDITIONS of books;articles worldwide.

*INNUMERABLE MAGAZINE & NEWSPAPER ARTICLES, STORIES, in top publications.
*MANY PERSONAL APPEARANCES, TV, RADIO, INTERVIEWS, LECTURES.
*ADVERTISING AGENCIES: former President, Vice President, Executive Staff.
*INSTRUCTOR AT NEW YORK UNIVERSITY and IONA COLLEGE -- writing, advertising.
 *INSTRUCTOR in MYSTERY WRITERS OF AMERICA writing courses.
*CARTOONIST *GAG WRITER *EDITOR, college and high school publications.
*Was NEWSPAPER REPORTER..TEXTILE LABORER..MILL FOREMAN..RETAIL CLERK.

SCHOOLING: Paterson NJ High School..Univ. of Pa...Columbia,NYU,New School.
HOMES: Paterson NJ; Allentown,Pa.; Grottoes,Va.; NYC; Mamaroneck, N.Y.

WIFE: Natalie, professional artist, teaches oil painting in home studio.
DAUGHTER: Dr. Wendy Baker Cammer, Ph. D. in Molecular Biology.
SON: Steven Jeffrey Baker; psychology, writer books, articles; editor.

 WRITING AIM: To help people live happier, more rewarding lives.

Figure 2

expert in this field. As you begin to specialize, there's no reason why you can't do what McCahill has done. Some editors, of course, don't particularly like it and will cut you out, but others will build you up because they know building writers and experts in their magazine also builds the magazine. The rule here seems to be, put yourself prominently in the central picture and make sure your name is on the caption. If at all possible, also put yourself in two or three more pictures in the same article. In these, you can do almost anything, but preferably be in action.

WORK YOURSELF INTO ARTICLE TITLES

Again, one of the best ways to get attention and make yourself known is to put your name in some of the article titles. Tom McCahill is a master at this. Here are some of the ways he's done it.

1. "Tom McCahill Revisits the Tornado"

2. "McCahill Tests the Mustang"

3. "McCahill Tests the Dodge"

4. "Tom McCahill's Contest: Win His Model 'A' Ford"

In addition, in *Mechanix Illustrated,* McCahill has a section in the index devoted exclusively to him. With this type of impact, how can you miss?

So, once in awhile when you're writing articles that lend themselves to this treatment, try throwing your name in the title and see what happens. This should probably be with a magazine you've been working for over a period of time; however, it should also be one in which you already have some reader identification.

Some editors, of course, won't let you get away with this —others will be delighted—and it will help to build your reputation.

GET YOUR NAME MENTIONED FREQUENTLY

This is probably a modified version of "I don't care what they say about me as long as they spell my name right."

Whenever possible, encourage the magazine to mention your name—whether it be in the mailbag, articles, editorials, or whatever.

One writer continually writes letters to the editor under an assumed name, commenting on his articles. The editor picks these up and prints one or two in every mailbag. Since readers read this section as much or more than the rest of the magazine, it continually keeps his name in circulation as a writer.

It is also possible to refer to yourself in the articles. Do this by letting somebody else call you by name.

In addition, you can often get the editor to mention you when you start a new series or a different type of article in his magazine. Sometimes he'll run a picture along with this mention (Figure 3).

HERE IS HOW TO BUILD AN IMAGE
IN A PARTICULAR MAGAZINE

The best way to build an image in a magazine is not do a smorgasbord of articles, but to do one particular series of articles with which you identify yourself over and over again. Within a year or so, the impact of this will begin to establish you with the readers of that magazine.

Now let's take some examples—I'll pull these out of the smaller magazines, since I think this is the easiest place to start and the easiest place to build an image—the rules, however, are the same for the larger ones.

A good example of image building with a select audience is the Faith Terry series in *Trailer Life*. Back in September of 1965, she and her huband started a group of articles called "Liveability Audit." This was simply a survey of a particular brand of trailer to determine the convenience or inconvenience of

Figure 3. Editors Will Mention Your Name.

Reprinted by permission of Trailer Life *magazine.*

HOW TO BUILD YOUR NAME FOR EXTRA PROFIT

living in it. This was introduced with the title "Introducing *T.L.'s* Liveability Audit."

These articles included pictures of Faith Terry doing the audit. In the December 1965 issue of *Trailer Life,* the Chinook Mobilodge shows Faith Terry examining a double sink, the dinette table, sitting and looking at the cabinets, and getting into the mobilodge. A caption identifies her by name. She uses "we" throughout which makes you keep thinking back to who the author is.

This same format appears in article after article, month after month. The impact basically is achieved through pictures of the author and the captions.

Another good example of this is Ted Trueblood in *Field and Stream.* This, of course, has been going on for some time and his name has been appearing on hunting and fishing articles for years—but the magazine even did a piece one time on "Is There a Real Ted Trueblood?"

LOCAL PUBLICITY ALSO HELPS

Speaking from a national sense, and from the standpoint of selling yourself to editors, local publicity probably is the worst. However, if you are looking for speech-writing ghosting jobs, brochures, pamphlets, or local companies' jobs, this can help. One of my writers is a master at this. Every time he makes a speech, he sends his picture with a little blurb about what he is going to do in to a number of local papers. This practically always gets picked up. In addition, if he's doing anything at all around town, he makes sure he gets plenty of publicity. He simply writes the news release, takes a few pictures, and sends it in to the local editor with "News Release" at the top. This invariably results in quite a bit of publicity for him.

For instance, he took the local boy scouts on a canoeing field trip down one of the rivers. The headline on this was "Local Writer Leads Scouts." In the story, he managed to work in some of his national credits and a few other details of his writing career.

He and a few other local writers put a few pieces of their work on display at one of the local libraries. You can believe this also got into print.

The rule is any time you do anything other people might be interested in reading about, by all means write your own news release, take an 8 × 10 glossy and send it in.

Here's an example of what a typical newspaper news release looks like.

Duane G. Newcomb
P. O. Box 618
Carmichael, California 95608
August 29, 1969

News Release for Immediate Release

FREE-LANCE WRITER WILL TALK TO CLUB

Duane Newcomb, author of over 2000 published articles, will be guest speaker at the Saturday 6:30 PM dinner meeting of the Sacramento branch of the California Writers Club at the El Rancho Motel in West Sacramento.

"Editors Buy Ideas, Not Writing" will be the theme of his talk.

Newcomb, who makes his living as a free-lance writer, aims his material at the whole scope of the magazine business. His talk is designed to show other writers how they can meet with success in this field.

He also teaches a popular writing course for the adult education division of American River College.

The dinner meeting is open to the public. Reservations may be made by calling Victoria Schwartz at 443-8740.

LET OTHER WRITERS HELP

In looking for publicity and getting your name out to editors and others who will buy your material, don't overlook the help fellow writers can give. This can be quite substantial.

For instance, Warren Smith, a writer in the Midwest, had an assignment from *Family Weekly* magazine to do an article on businessmen and others using private planes. Now Warren knew that Frank Zdy (a well-known trade journal writer) uses a private plane in a sideline of his as a business consultant and also in flying around to his business writing assignments. He called Frank, interviewed him for 30 minutes, then used him as one of his examples in the *Family Weekly* feature.

Result, Frank Zdy got national publicity and his name before several million readers—many who undoubtedly can be useful in building his name and also in advancing his career.

In another case, a student of mine, Ray Mackaman, started out to write for company magazines and wound up as a photographer specializing in construction—his clients were the advertising departments of many huge corporations.

Ray, in the course of his work, set up a small 13-foot trailer as a darkroom. At the time, I was working for *Trailer Life* magazine and decided this would be a good article. I looked the trailer over, got a few of his unusual experiences on construction jobs, took a few pictures in the trailer, picked up a few on the job, and wrote an article about Ray entitled "Trailering Photographer."

Ray had reprints made and sent them out to every one of his clients, plus a great many potential clients. The result: many clients wrote him, telling him how great the story was. Some he hadn't heard from in months sent assignments—others who had been giving him assignments regularly started giving more —we estimated the total amount of business from this article ran just right around $4000.

DON'T OVERLOOK ARTICLES IN WRITERS' MAGAZINES

Actually, you'll get more publicity here with other writers than you will with editors. But it does help build your name as an expert. And anything you can do will be read avidly. For instance, I did an article for *Writer's Digest* some time ago on how to write new product releases. I'm still getting phone calls on it eight years later and I've also had editors mention it to me several times.

BUILD YOUR OWN AUDIENCE

The more you're known in a particular field, and the more the editor knows his readers want to read your work, the more money you can command. How much depends on how good a job you've done. But simply because you're in demand you can ask more and probably get it.

In one of the conversations I had with Erle Stanley Gardner, he said that one of the most important things for a writer to do is build his name. You may never be an Erle Stanley Gardner, but you can be so well known in the field by building yourself, that you will be able to demand far better rates than the average writer. The easiest way to do this is to identify yourself with a particular field. One writer decided that boating was his field. He started modestly, writing articles whenever possible for the boating magazines. He then established a column in one with his picture. Shortly afterward, he set up a question and answer column in the same magazine to answer readers' technical questions. He also started selling general boating articles to the major magazines and came out with three boating books which he referred to in his own articles. In addition, these books were written up in the magazine he worked for. The result of all this concentration: readers began associating him with the field and started watching for his articles and writing to him for advice.

Another example of this (and I don't know whether it's deliberate or not) is writer V. Lee Oretle. Say "Recreational Vehicles" and this is the first name that pops into the mind of a lot of enthusiasts . . . . his articles appear in many trailer magazines. It's also almost impossible to pick up *Popular Science* or *Popular Mechanics* during the summer outdoor months without running into this name. His articles are so technical and information-oriented that they automatically tend to make readers look to him as an expert. Some of his titles are "How to Select a Pickup Truck for Camper Duty," "The Amazing Evolution of Modern Pickups," and "Roundup of Trucks." Does this sound complicated? It isn't: here are some ABC's.

1. *Concentrate on a field in which you can become an expert*— for example: recreational vehicles, houseboating, family problems, skin diving, handling children, and others.

2. *Start with just a few articles in one magazine*—spread throughout the field as quickly as possible, then try a few pieces in this field for general magazines.

3. *Get columns started as quickly as possible*—concentrate on one magazine and begin to establish yourself there using the other publicity ideas explained in this chapter.

4. *Make sure, when possible, your articles contain a blurb on your qualifications as an expert in the field*—also make sure each column uses your pictures.

5. *After you have been in the field for several years, try to add books in your specialty*—sometimes magazine publishers will help. Be sure and ask the magazines you're working for. Also query other possible publishers in these fields.

Checking on Chapter 12

Building your name to the point where it's recognized by a number of readers means additional money. Here are some tips:

1. *Use blurbs and pictures with as many articles as possible. These should include your qualifications in the field.*

2. *Pictures help identify you. Put yourself in your own article pictures when possible. Captions identify you by name.*

3. *Try putting your name in the title. This is a simple method, yet putting your name in a title has a tremendous impact.*

4. *Make sure your name is mentioned whenever possible, in letters, in articles, in editorials, and whenever else possible.*

5. *Build your image with a series of articles on the same subject. Be sure to use pictures at every step.*

6. *Try local publicity—articles in writer's magazines help—so does mention by other writers.*

7. *Try building your own audience. You can do this in the following ways:*

   a. *Concentrate on a particular field that will let you become an expert.*
   b. *Concentrate on spreading your articles on one subject across a particular field of magazines.*
   c. *Try to establish columns.*
   d. *Make sure you use all possible publicity techniques to build your name.*
   e. *Add books when possible.*

CHAPTER 13

How to Hit
the Bigger Markets

Never be satisfied with the money you're getting. It seems strange, but part of each year's writing income is strictly mental. I, myself, find I'm often able to double my income without even changing magazines. All I do is decide I want more money. Working in the business and specialty fields a lot as I do, I know there are many articles that will bring $30, $50, $80, or less if you let them. Sometimes I drift into this trap and suddenly realize I'm only averaging $60 or $70 an article. The way I get out is to simply decide that every article from then on must average at least $100 (or whatever I want). I then begin to be very selective, turning down assignments which are lower than this, and asking $100, $150, $200, or more for every piece.

One time Frank Zdy and writer Chet Cunningham were discussing the "truck talk" columns Chet turns out for many magazines. Frank said to Chet, "If you want to make more money instead of soliciting more magazines, why not ask your accounts for a raise?" The results were several thousands of dollars more income without any additional work.

In another case, I automatically marked down "article price $100" at the end of one of my queries for a ski business magazine. When I picked up the magazine, I noticed the large number of ads carried and decided this was silly. I changed the price to $150 and didn't hear a whimper.

One time on one of these "money binges," I started asking for what I considered outlandish sums for trade journal work —$200, $300, $400, and $500. Strangely enough, I started getting it. One magazine I asked for $125 ($75 more than I'd been told I could get), wrote back and offered $175.

The same is true when you're going from low-pay markets to bigger ones. The first thing you must start with is a big dissatisfaction with the amounts you're making (or the type of work you're doing). Then start reaching out toward bigger magazines and more money. Start looking at the bigger magazines with an eye to what you can actually do for them. Then start writing queries to these magazines asking for what you want.

I see this idea work all the time in my classes. One student told me he wouldn't accept less than $200 per article ever again. From that day on he began writing queries to the big magazines in his field—*Field and Stream, Sports Afield,* and others. Now he didn't sell every time to these magazines, but occasionally he'd hit one and some of the minors that paid fairly well. Even in the beginning his checks averaged $200 or more. After he learned the fundamentals of selling, he simply ignored the other markets and struck out toward the ones that he knew paid well. Another student aiming at the $2000 level found he had the same experience.

SPIN LOWER MARKET MATERIAL OFF TO
MAJOR MAGAZINES—HERE'S HOW

Frank Zdy of San Diego is undoubtedly the top trade journal (business) writer in the country today. Frank, for years, has worked for a magazine called *Auto Laundry News.* This magazine goes to owners and managers of car washes and includes such articles as "How to Get More Business," "How to Merchandise Better," etc. Over the years, Frank has written several hundred articles for this magazine and knows the field inside and out.

Now that seems like a difficult consumer magazine subject but it isn't. Frank got to looking at the automotive articles in *Better Homes and Gardens* and decided maybe they'd be interested. He wrote a query asking the editor if he'd like a piece on "How to Get the Most Out of Your Full-Service Car Wash." The answer was yes.

This is a good example of how to spin off material you're already doing in the lower markets for some of the better paying ones.

The trick, I believe, is to take a look at what you're doing, then decide if some of the better paying magazines would be interested in your subject. After this, look over several issues of each magazine you want to hit and try to come up with an angle on the material you're working with that would fit. Next write a query or outline, send it in, and sit back and wait.

HITTING THE BIG MAGAZINES MEANS
KNOWING THEM WELL

Probably one of the biggest tricks to hitting larger magazines regularly is to know them and their audiences like the back of your hand. Here again is where you should analyze the advertising. Try to place your audience down to their income, religious preferences, and much more.

TRY TO BECOME FAMILIAR WITH ARTICLE TYPES
HIGH PAYING MAGAZINES ARE BUYING

We have talked about this before but now we must do better. Always try to give the magazine ideas as close to their needs as possible. The more you can hit a bull's-eye here, the more the editors will buy. This means, of course, that you should sit down with 12 issues of any major magazine you want to hit and go over it carefully, looking for the topics they're using plus the treatment they're giving to each topic.

After you've been doing this awhile, you'll begin to get the feel of what the magazines handle and will know immediately whether your idea will fit or not.

If we look at *Family Circle's* Table of Contents, for instance, we'll see they take articles about home furnishings, food, home equipment, creative crafts, beauty, child care, health, and others.

Unfortunately, most of their home furnishings, food, home equipment, fashions, etc. are staff done. But their articles on the family, child care, and health are often free-lanced, so we want to look closer here.

In recent issues we find: "Olympic Champion Bill Toomey Tells Young People What Winning's All About," "Mother Knows Best, for Family and You," "How to Achieve Parent Power" by Dr. Haim Ginott, "After My Second Child Arrived" (differences between children), "What Makes Children Cheat?", and more.

In short, they use thoroughly comprehensive articles about you and your children—usually some universal parent's problem.

Category two is health, so let's look at some of these being run. (1) "How I Answer My Patients' Questions About the Pill"; (2) "When Should Children Have Cosmetic Surgery?"; (3) "About Pap Testing–It Might Save Your Life"; (4) "Sub-Zero Surgery–Medicine's New Knifeless Techniques."

There is a little emphasis on the new—but basically it tries to answer questions about medical problems that really concern you.

SUGGEST ARTICLES THAT FIT INTO THE FORMAT

In offering articles to this or any other major magazine, then, we want to take into account what they're already doing and try to decide how to fit into their format with our ideas.

Let's take child care again. In looking at what they've done, we realize *Family Circle* pays attention to problems every family has and tries to offer solutions.

We should sit down then and think of some of the common problems and maybe the not-so-common ones that plague us and see if we can come up with some answers that tie in. Notice that they use "you" to tie directly to the reader.

One of the problems I can think of is the experience of going to school for the first time. There's an adjustment here that's sometimes traumatic. We might try that out with the title, "You Can Help Your Child Adjust to School."

Now here are some other possibilities: "What If Your Child Doesn't Want to Go to Church?" "Ways to Help Your Underachievers," and "How to Handle a Rebel." See if you can add your own.

For the medical or health group, do the same thing. Migraine headaches, for instance, are a problem that affects many people and might make a *Family Circle* article. But to stay with what they're doing, we can't just offer migraines—it must be something really useful. Perhaps here we could offer the title, "You Can Get Relief from Migraines," then, in the article, emphasize the problem—what causes migraines, what the new discoveries are, and what can now be done to gain relief.

STUDY THE BIG MAGAZINES CAREFULLY—
A GUIDE TO MAGAZINE ANALYZING

You'll find the larger magazines a little more difficult to hit and a little more concerned with actual writing than the minors. Therefore, you are going to have to turn in articles that are really professional and really match their style. This means you must analyze style carefully even more so than for the general markets. You'll also have to go over these magazines as we have with our other analyzing—looking at the editorials, the ads, the articles, and more.

I suggest here that you use this form we developed some time ago for additional analysis.

Analysis Guide

1. Name, publisher, editor, where published:

   _____

2. From the Table of Contents, list the types of material used and the approximate percentages taken: _____

   _____

3. What do you think your chances are of selling to these magazines? _____

4. What types of features are used—personality— personal experience—utility—interview article— or what? _____

   _____

5. How are the pictures handled? What kinds of illustrations? _____

   _____

6. Article length? _____

7. What peculiarities of style—direct address— formula—talky—or what? _____

   _____

---

8. Are most articles first, second, or third person?

_____

9. What kinds of leads are used most? _____

_____

10. Are the writers known or unknown? _____

_____

In addition to doing a more careful magazine analysis you should also try to be as familiar as possible with the way the articles are put together. This means you should try to learn basically how an editor wants individual articles handled.

You don't have to make a tremendous project out of this, but one of the things we've learned to do in class is once in a while break apart one of the articles in the magazine you want to hit to make sure you're on target. This procedure is quite simple. It consists simply of numbering the paragraphs, deciding what each paragraph says, where the anecdotes are, about what percentage the writer devoted to statistics, how much he relies on authorities, and, in short, just how he put it together.

It's possible, of course, to parallel an article using their format. I don't recommend this, but if you're completely unsure of yourself, this will give you a guide to follow that will put you pretty close to the one they're using.

Now do it this way:

1. Number the paragraphs of the article you want to analyze.

2. Write a brief paragraph outline on a separate sheet of paper.

3. Note which paragraphs contain dialogue, which include statistics, and so on. When finished, you'll have a pretty good idea of this article's composition and can make sure yours roughly contains all these elements.

WHAT TO INCLUDE IN MAJOR MAGAZINE QUERIES

Like all queries, a query to a major market is a selling letter and should be restricted if possible to one page. This letter should simply hook your editor, get in and get out, and ask him for the sale. Include no more than necessary for an editor to make an intelligent decision.

Basically, a query contains these points:

1. Hook.
2. Angle or title.
3. Why subject is important and what it is.
4. What you want in your article.
5. A line asking for the sale.

(1) First you'll want to hook the editor into the query. You can do this with a brief, snappy statement that says, for instance, "Would you like to make an extra $5000 on your summer vacation . . . ?", or "Here's something I think you'll like . . .", or any similar statement that is short, catches attention, and leads on into the body of your query.

(2) You should immediately give the editor the angle you're going to present. The easiest way to do this, I find, is to give the title and simply say, "Suggested Piece On: . . . ." and either put the title or angle here in six to 15 words. This gets the idea across immediately.

(3) You should explain a little about your subject here but keep it short. Let the editor know why it's important to his readers and, if possible, indicate also in this part what your sources are and if pictures are available.

(4) Here you should tell the editor what five or six points you're going to put in your article. I like to put this at the end and simply list in one sentence exactly what I'm going to do. Let's say we're doing an article on how to build a table. In the end sentence, I'll simply say, "In this article I'll go into why you should build the table, the history of the table, some of the

possible uses, the materials, the tools, and how to put it together."

(5) I always feel it's important to ask for the sale at the end. Do this by saying, "Let me know about this," or "If you're interested, I'll be glad to do this piece," or something similar.

In addition to those points, you should also include these additional items:

(a) What's been done on the subject. With major magazines, this is important. Go back the past ten years in *Readers' Guide to Periodical Literature* and find out.

(b) An introduction to yourself—if the editor doesn't know you, give him your writing credentials.

(c) And finally, although I don't consider this major, refer in your query to something an editor has done in the past in his own magazine. If you say, "This article will be similar to 'How to Top Tulips' in your July issue and cover approximately the same points," the editor then knows you're more or less familiar with his magazine as to style and content.

Now let's look at a query and see how this is done.

Mr. Alexander Suczek
Friends Magazine
Department FM 3-135 General Motors Bldg.
Detroit 2, Michigan

Dear Mr. Suczek

Here's something I think you'll like.

What I want to suggest is a piece on: STEAM IS BACK—Shades of the Wild West.

Many of us dream of the old West, but Norm Clark, President

---

of the Roaring Camp and Big Trees Narrow-Gauge Railroad has gone out and done something about it.

Decrying the fact that "steam is disappearing," Clark got together an authentic collection of steam locomotives (and rolling stock) from the 1800's and erected almost an entire "country" on a 177-acre preserve near Felton, California.

Roaring Camp itself is planned to represent California from 1848 to 1888 with a stagecoach line, general store, harness shop, etc., all as they appeared during this time. Commercialism has been kept to a minimum. And every visitor must park his car at Felton and take the narrow-gauge railroad through the virgin redwoods.

Designed as an authentic piece of Americana, this project is a favorite of railroad buffs as well as the general public, and has caught the imagination of many in central California.

In this piece, I'd like to go into some of the locomotives and rolling stock (its history, where it operated, etc.), how it is being authenticated, just how it can be reached, and some of the other colorful details.

Let me know on this.

I will provide either black-and-white photos or color (or both).

Cordially,

This query follows the plan pretty well—it more or less hooks (1), gives the angle (2), tells what the subject is, why it's important, and of interest to the reader (3), briefly tells what the author wants to do (4), and asks for the sale (5).

It also lets the editor know the writer can provide pictures. It does not, however, give the writer's credits, tell the editor what's been done, or refer back to his magazine—whether you do this or not depends on the magazine and whether or not you, as a writer, are known to the editor.

BREAKING THE PSYCHOLOGICAL BARRIER

Somehow, writers, like everybody else, seem to get in a rut. I know business and specialty writers who've gone to $20,000-$25,000 a year and can't seem to get beyond. They also feel like there's a solid barrier between them and bigger markets that they somehow can't get across. This, of course, is sheer nonsense.

Cracking the bigger markets regularly simply means better knowledge of what they're taking and a better job of focusing in, but basically the principles are the same.

The secret here, I find, is to try!

One method I've found works well in class is to have my students collect the last 12 issues of the top 40 magazines. Then go over a single magazine as we did before, trying to relate what they know or are doing to what's appearing . . . . usually they break the articles over a year into categories, and try to find something within those categories the magazine might be interested in.

Ordinarily a study of 12 issues will trigger two or three possible ideas. The students then sit down and query—in the meantime, studying other magazines with the same idea in mind. When my students are making a concentrated effort to crack these markets, I have them go over all magazines once every two or three months looking for ideas.

The key is actually doing it. This is why most writers have problems. It takes the action of sitting down and studying 12 issues, coming up with two or three ideas regularly, querying, and keeping at it until you actually hit. After that it's simply a matter of building the magazine as a regular market by the methods we've already gone through. Once you have three or four magazines as regulars, the rest is fairly easy.

Checking on Chapter 13

Never be satisfied with what you're making. Keep looking for markets that pay more. In addition, ask for what you consider outlandish. Sometime try doubling your rates to a regular market.

Try to spin off material into higher markets. Once you've finished an article for the low-pay markets, go over the higher paying ones to see if some aspects of what you've already researched and written can't be done for more money—sometimes you can get two or three additional sales this way.

Magazine study is always the key. Try to determine exactly what the larger magazines are taking and how they want their material handled—then offer it to them.

Study the types of material the better markets are taking. Break it up into categories, practice putting your ideas into these categories.

Major magazine queries should contain these elements: (1) The idea in a nutshell; (2) what your idea is all about; (3) why the editor or his readers should be interested; (4) what you're going to include; (5) what's been done on the subject; (6) your credits—or why you're qualified to write the story—what research or picture sources are available; (7) if it's important, refer to something an editor has done in his own magazine.

Break the major market barrier by simply doing it. Go over 12 issues of a magazine you want to hit—develop several ideas and query!

CHAPTER 14

How to Keep Increasing Your Income and Build a Solid Success

No matter how good you are, no matter how many articles you can produce, and no matter how terrific your research is, you will not make big money until you have built some type of a reputation and until a significant number of editors know you can turn out quality material. Until this happens, editors just won't give out assignments—which form the basis for building volume and a big-money income.

The only possible way to build your reputation is simply to start writing. In the beginning, even though you specialize, try to build as wide a range of magazines as possible. Sometimes you might want to be writing more or less regularly for 40, 50, 60, or more. This probably means you won't be doing more than one or two articles a year for individual magazines, but it will let a lot of editors see what you can do. In the meantime, of course, try to get as many blurbs and special references to yourself as possible so your name will spread to other editors.

The second part of building your reputation is quality. There's an old axiom—give a little more than necessary—and this holds true in building your reputation and making editors want your work. It consists of several things. In the first place, you should keep striving for good, lucid organization—try to use solid words that really communicate, and attempt to say them as straightforwardly and clearly as possible. To do this, you must keep improving this part of your writing. The chapters in Rudolf Flesch on "How to Save Words," "How to Put Punch in Your Writing" will help you give the editor top-quality writing.

The third thing you should do is make sure your manuscripts are extremely neat and well set up. While a lot of the writers say that editors don't care what a manuscript looks like, this isn't true. This is the old school thing. If your composition is neat and clean, that's about 90 per cent of the battle. While it's not quite that simple, part of the job is making it look good. If the editor sees a number of errors, cross-outs, and sloppy erasures on the first few pages, he's liable to assume you're a sloppy craftsman and will do a bad overall job.

Here is the way a manuscript should be set up: (Pg. 223) . In addition, providing photographs is a convenience to editors and a way to earn extra money—but not a requirement. Even if you do not provide photographs with your article, many editors have outside sources and some even maintain elaborate photo files of their own.

If you're taking your own pictures, two finished sizes are acceptable: 5×7 and 8×10 single-weight glossy. Always make sure they're sharp and have good contrast. Editors, of course, all pay extra for the photographs you provide (from $5 each up).

In addition, editors often will pay standard rates for photos you provide from other sources. (For a complete list, see Chapter 5.)

Mr. Duane G. Newcomb
1010 Ash Street
Anywhere, U. S. A. 95124

(Approximately
1400 Words)

EFFECTIVE ORGANIZATION—KEY TO SUCCESS

by

Duane Newcomb

I once heard a successful businessman say, "Nine times out of ten when one of our company projects fails, it's due to poor organization. If I could send all my executives back to school for just one course, this would be it."

The same statement could very well be applied to all of us. After all, no matter who we are: students, college or business school graduates, or businessmen, we're continually faced with the job of organizing something.

Now this might seem difficult. But believe me, it isn't. And no matter what we're talking about: a sales campaign, putting together a Sahara supply . . . .

We won't go into photography here, but try always to send top-quality work. If you're taking your own, study the magazine's photographs as religiously as you study the magazine itself. See what the editor wants. Does he want people posed? Does he want candid shots? Does he want people in action, or what? After you find out, by all means give it to him.

Always do as good work as you can and keep improving on appearance, on tightness and readability, on manuscript organization, and on the type of pictures you turn in.

MAKE SURE YOU HAVE A SUCCESS ATTITUDE

Article writing is like any other field. There are an awful lot of disappointments as you go along. You'll find times when one rejection slip will spoil an entire day. Napoleon Hill and W. Clement Stone in their book, *Success Through a Positive Mental Attitude*,[1] talk about the part positive mental attitude (PMA) plays in success. This is exactly what you need to be an article writer.

It helps, of course, if you set some sort of a goal. Decide now that you're going to be a full-time writer, or you're going to eventually make $30,000 a year, or more—then know that you'll get there. Cardinal rule number 1—never, never give up!

Napoleon Hill and W. Clement Stone also have a saying in their book that every adversity has the seed of a greater benefit— and there's nothing truer in article writing than this.

Know you're going to succeed and never give up. Every time you get a rejection, know this really is a step towards your goal and that you're simply building your career.

Suppose, for instance, you do an article on the use of electronic data processing in the hardware business and it's rejected—a loss of both time and money. Stop—nothing's lost because you build an electronic data processing background that will show up as you go along.

---

[1] Napoleon Hill and W. Clement Stone, *Success Through a Positive Mental Attitude* (Englewood Cliffs, N.J.: Prentice-Hall, Inc., 1960).

WRITERS' ORGANIZATIONS HELP

You can gain great advantages from writers' organizations —but only the right ones. As your career progresses, you'll discover there are many, many writers' clubs and organizations. The question, of course, is can they help? The answer is some will help tremendously. Others will slow you down.

In the first place, there are the local groups that meet weekly or monthly in your area. Now there are, undoubtedly, exceptions, but basically they consist primarily of would-be writers, or fiction writers, or people dabbling at writing (or maybe they've even sold three or four articles or stories)— primarily, however, they get together because they like writers and like to talk "writing."

If you want to socialize—fine. But remember, that's all you're doing. As career advancement, most of these groups are a waste of time.

Similarly, there are several national groups consisting mostly of amateurs or people who've sold two or three articles and are just splashing around trying to write. These organizations are also a waste of time. Some have large memberships, but unless they're really working toward making writing a profession, have a number of the top-notch writers, and are trying to do a job of career building, they'll do you little good.

Now let's look at some constructive ones.

Several organizations are extremely worthwhile. Most useful are: (1) American Society of Journalists and Authors, (2) Associated Business Writers of America, (3) Outdoor Writers' Association of America, (4) Society of American Travel Writers, (5) National Association of Science Writers.

American Society of Journalists and Authors, 1501 Broadway, Rm. 1907, New York, NY 10036, consists of approximately 250 top working writers across the country, turning out about 75 to 90 per cent of everything you see in the major magazines. The organization maintains a New York office and publishes a monthly newsletter. Major magazines often assign articles to these members and consider them a prime source of people who can really turn out the material.

The Society publishes a regular newsletter which contains market and other information, plus a listing of rates—paid members. Membership requirements are six articles in major magazines or one book during the preceding 12 months.

Associated Business Writers of America, 1450 S. Havana, Suite 620, Aurora CO 80012—I've belonged to this organization for a number of years and consider it excellent. Membership consists of about 150 members and associates (members are full time, associates may hold jobs), many are top professionals recognized by business magazine editors as the best. The organization publishes a monthly bulletin and a yearly directory. Directories are carried on the desks of many editors who use them in making assignments. Membership requirements are professional quality writing and active engagement in the trade journal field.

Outdoor Writers' Association of America, 4141 W. Bradley Rd., Milwaukee, WI 53209—this organization has some 1100 members who are newspaper and magazine writers, editors, photographers, broadcasters, and others. Publications include a monthly newsletter, *Outdoors Unlimited,* an annually revised *Directory of Outdoor Writers* and *Communicating the Outdoor Experience.*

Society of American Travel Writers, 1120 Connecticut Ave. N. W., Washington, DC 20036, consists of editors, newspaper writers, freelance writers, and others who earn most of their living from travel writing. This is an organization of professionals. To join, you must maintain a steady flow of published material.

National Association of Science Writers, Inc. Box 294, Greenlawn, NY 11740, currently has about 270 members reporting scientific and technological developments through newspapers, magazines, radio, and TV—also about 400 associate members who represent special scientific interests such as universities.

BOOK CREDITS INCREASE YOUR WORTH

Ever look at the bottom of an article and see a little notation which says, "Tommy Rider is the author of the book 'How to Build Automobiles in Your Backyard' "? Sure you have. It helps give the article credence and also marks the author as an authority. The more backup like this, the more readership you pick up—and the more in demand your knowledge is by readers, the more you can ask for your work. Now, admittedly, book credits are not going to bring you a big increase, but you can certainly ask 5 to 10 per cent above what you would normally expect.

George Wells, for instance, a highly successful outdoor writer and editor of *Camping Guide* and other outdoor publications, has a number of books on camping and outdoor activities. When negotiating with *McCall's Magazine* for a travel article, the editors indicated to him that they wanted his name because he was a known authority in the field.

HOW TO CRACK THE BOOK MARKET

As you go along, books should become a part of your regular writing income. But unless you find you're especially suited to this, you'll probably want to divide your overall income between magazine articles and books, with magazine articles occupying much of your time.

The reason is, of course, that articles are faster—faster to write, faster to research, and faster to cash in on. Properly handled, however, books can really help swell your income especially after you're going really well.

Primarily you go about getting a book in print the same way you do an article. You first (1) slant your book for the market you intend to hit, you (2) sell it to the publisher before you write a word, and you (3) sign a contract.

Now let's look at how one free-lancer does it. First of all, she decides on an idea—this might be on *credit, art,* a *how-to,* or something else—then she goes to the *Subject Guide to Books in Print* in the library and looks up all the books on her subject. Next, using this, the *Writer's Market,* plus publishers' catalogs she's sent for, she lists all the potential buyers for her book.

Book publishers are like magazines, of course, in that they have individual preferences for the type of work they publish— and like the magazines, you should study your publishers and try to learn what kind of books they publish and how they like the material handled.

This same writer then sits down and sends out a regular query letter to several publishers . . . . this is basically a magazine-type query except it's usually one page, single-spaced —it presents the project, gives the reasons why it's a good subject right now, and tells about the writer's qualifications.

When a publisher expresses interest, she makes up a prospectus (a long query), a table of contents (outline), and two sample chapters, and offers it to one publisher at a time. On the basis of this, she gets a contract.

Here are some steps:

1. Make up a query similar to the magazine queries in Chapter 13, but include why you're qualified to do this book . . . . let the publisher know that if he's interested you'll send an outline, a table of contents, and two sample chapters.

2. When a publisher expresses interest, send a prospectus. I've seen these handled many ways, with the prospectus running many pages. I prefer to do a two- or three-page prospectus, which tells in the first two or three sentences the theme of the book, makes the point, tells why it's important—often using examples—backs this up with a few statistics and quotes from authorities, then gets down to cases by telling exactly what's going into the book. Ordinarily this is fairly detailed. If this is backed up with a table of contents, of course, it's even stronger.

HOW TO WORK WITH AN AGENT

In building income and your career, an agent can be quite helpful. I, personally, believe that you shouldn't even begin to look for an agent until you are approaching the $15,000 or $20,000 a year figure. You certainly don't need one for the specialty magazines . . . . and even in the larger magazines it's not vital. No agent can do better than you can with a good query and the follow-through suggested in this book.

What then can an agent do? . . . . two things: (1) He can help you with your marketing once you're turning out salable material. Good agents are on top of the market—they see editors and publishers all the time and often know what they're looking for. (2) Often he can also do a better negotiating job than you can.

Now, how do you find an agent? . . . . there are several ways: 1. Editors will sometimes recommend an agent—if you've made several sales to major magazines, ask for a list of several agents they deal with. 2. Your writer friends may recommend you to their own agents—this is usually a pretty good way. 3. You can send for a list of agents from the Society of Authors' Representatives, 101 Park Ave., New York, NY 10017, and write to several telling them about the type of work you do.

Remember, however, good agents are busy and they want only the writers who will pay off—as a result, I, again, recommend not even trying until you get to the point where you're working in the major magazine market and book field and need someone to take the business side off your hands.

Now, just how do you work with an agent—there are, of course, as many ways as there are writers, but I suggest it's up to you to do the work.

As an example, one well-known writer sets aside time each day to study the major magazines and to think up ideas to tie in with what they're doing . . . . from this he comes up with three or four queries a month which are shot off to his agent. In addition, he spends an equal amount of time studying *Publishers' Weekly* to keep track of the books that are being published. He also keeps a notebook in which all major publishers are listed with the books they're publishing, under subject categories . . . . a glance tells him what topics are being pushed

. . . . and by following *Publishers' Weekly* he keeps up fairly well with how they're selling.

This means, then, that he's pretty well on top of what's going on in the magazine and book business, and anything he suggests is likely to fit in. He also knows as well as his agent, who's likely to buy what. Why does he use an agent then? He does so because his agent just adds that much more knowledge to what he's already accumulated, and between them they often come up with just the right topic at the right time for top money. In addition, the agent takes the problem of negotiating off this writer's hands so he can spend more time at actual writing.

COLUMNS HELP MAKE YOUR WRITING SUCCESS MORE SOLID

I won't promise you that editors are going to pay more money because you're writing columns, but your success base, or sustaining income, is certainly going to be higher when you have several solid columns behind you. They, of course, will also get your name out to more editors and let it be known that you are an expert in particular fields. This never hurts and will enable you to obtain easy go-aheads in the field of your column since the editor knows your work will be authoritative. As a result, of course, you can ask just a little more for these articles. A good example of a writer who has used columns to build a success base is Chet Cunningham of San Diego. Chet's idea was that he would take the same column and do it for a number of magazines in noncompeting fields. The columns were tailored for each particular editor in this way. If they were going to florist magazines, he'd talk about florists, if automotive stores, he'd talk about automotive stores, etc.

Chet then picked a subject which he felt would have a wide appeal and which he knew a great deal about. His topic, "Truck Talk," appears in about 20 trade publications across the country. It's roughly an 800-word column which discusses truck problems—maintenance, repair, how to get the most out of your truck fleet, and a number of other items. Chet charges from $30 to $50 each, and has built a base of about $1000 a month.

In the beginning, his columns were started by writing the editor suggesting the idea. Sample columns were then sent to interested editors. Chet also insists that there are a number of fields where this same thing could be done, including advertising, promotion, merchandising, display, credit, and others.

SUSTAINING ARTICLES AND SEVERAL-PART SERIES BUILD INCOME

As you go along, you'll realize that digging up new assignments every month really keeps you scrambling. If, in your queries, you can get editors to assign two- or three-part series or articles that go on and on, your income will increase almost automatically.

A good example of this is a sustaining series I have going in *Camper Coachman Magazine*. In the beginning, we decided to do a series on State Park systems in every state in the United States. These were designed to explore the history of that particular system, talk about what there is to see, and then detail a number of outstanding parks. The price for each was $100 and if we did every state—50 states—the series would run a little over four years. Think of the time you'd waste if you'd have to write 50 $100 queries to generate $5000.

Free-lance writer, William Hector, has done this successfully for such magazines as *Popular Mechanics, Popular Science,* and *Science and Mechanics*.

Hector got into this more or less by accident—taking an adult education class in mechanics, he found the instructor started to repeat at the end of the first semester, and he also found that the automotive service handbooks were way ahead of him. He reasoned that there were thousands of people in that in-between area like himself. As a result, he decided to solicit one of the mechanics magazines on an automotive service series.

He then approached Wayne C. Leckey, Shops and Crafts editor, of *Popular Mechanics,* and started the series with four or five articles. At the time, he did not have the background, but felt that he could research material adequately and it'd be cumulative as he went along. Wayne C. Leckey, Shops and Crafts editor of *Popular Mechanics,* immediately bought the idea and asked for four or five articles in advance. Hector proceeded to send in 15 subjects, and all were accepted. The first check for this *Popular Mechanics* series was $180—before long, he was getting $300.

Now here are some simple rules to follow in deciding which series to submit and how you should go about it:

(1) Sit down with 12 issues of the magazine you're thinking of doing a series for, and start looking for blanks.

For instance, with *Trailer Life Magazine,* I noticed a number of letters to the editors talking about retirement and full-time trailering. There was very little being done at that time in magazines, so I suggested a column on retirement. This was accepted, then changed to "Full-Time Trailering ".

Ask yourself, what do these readers want to know that's not now being provided? . . . . go over and over the magazine until you know it backwards and forwards . . . . try to put yourself in the reader's place . . . . and each time try to think up at least two possible columns or series that this reader might be interested in.

(2) When you have come up with a number of ideas, pick out the one you think is best—then write a query outlining why you think their readers would be interested, what your series is about, and how you expect to handle it. Be sure, also, to put in there why you're qualified to do the series.

MORE COMPLICATED ARTICLES
MEAN MORE MONEY

The more complicated an article is, the more money it should bring.

For instance, years ago I used to do a number of articles for *Harvest Years,* a magazine in the retirement field for which I averaged about $80. Then I got an assignment to do a comprehensive look at the mobile home field . . . . its benefits to retirees, how to select a home, what were the best homes, etc. In this, I went into complete detail, including lists of what to look for, lists of manufacturers, and a great deal more. For this article, I received $200 instead of the usual $80.

Another example in my own background is a piece I did in the business field for *Home and Auto Retailer.* Ordinarily I get about $100 apiece for their articles. This one, however, was a detailed camping roundup. I went into how home and auto stores all over the country merchandised camping equipment, and also included extras on fishing boats, recreational vehicles, camping foods, and a lot more, adding detail after detail. This one drew close to $400.

When I talk about $70 or $400 for more complicated articles, this may not seem like much money. And it isn't individually. But I'm not talking about working on an individual basis. I'm talking about a whole approach that really adds up. Material from your $70 article, for instance, may be put together with a little more information to turn out your $400 piece.

Start cutting corners and begin increasing what you're getting for your total time, and suddenly you find yourself making a big-money monthly and weekly income.

The same principles apply to $1000 major magazine articles. These can easily be parlayed into more money by taking a more extensive approach.

When you expect to do extra work, such as this, and want more money, you'll ordinarily have to negotiate. It pays to tell the editor just what you have to do and exactly what you need for it. Articles like this can often increase your income considerably—and if you've done a number of articles in the general field and have good information in your files, it may take very little extra work.

YOU CAN GET EXPENSES

Many writers learn the hard way. For years I used to drive 100 to 200 miles for articles, pay for my own meals, and just chalk the expenses off to the cost of gathering material. Then I began to look around and discovered that others were doing the same thing for the same magazine, but were getting air fare, meals, hotels, 10 cents a mile travel expenses, and a number of other concessions. I suddenly realized I was being extremely silly. In actuality a writer makes little enough profit on his articles. By accounting costs over a period of time, I found that practically 50 per cent of every article is basic expenses, not profit as some editors like to tell you. Your living expenses, of course, must come out of the remaining 50 per cent. Therefore, costs, such as travel and motels, which have nothing to do with keeping up your writing operation, should be billed to the magazine.

Shortly after this discovery, I then began to add expenses to every article—and nine times out of ten I got them.

If an editor called on an assignment, I'd say, "Fine, that will be $100, and the trip is 200 miles at 10 cents a mile." This didn't seem to surprise anybody and it became standard procedure. This also includes telephone calls, meals, and anything else necessary.

Magazines are notorious, of course, for not wanting to pay their full share of the load. But in my opinion, no writer should let them get away with this. This is a legitimate expense and if it doesn't come out of their pocket, it comes out of yours. In effect, it means that you're paying part of their cost of doing business. And this just isn't fair. Big magazines, by the way, are just as much a violator of this as small ones.

ALWAYS KEEP PUSHING

By this, I mean always keep pushing for more money. Do this in a number of ways. First, by getting more for the work you're doing, and second, by continually looking for assignments which pay more.

After you've done ten or 15 articles for a magazine, I suggest you write and tell them expenses have gone up and you need a little more. Now you can leave it up to them how much more, or you can ask for what you want. You'll find that many magazines will go for a slight increase, say 10 or 15 per cent, and that's just that much more for the same amount of work.

In addition, of course, your operation should be in a continuous state of flux. This means you should continually search for markets that pay more. When you query, always ask for a little more than you think you can get.

Now let's see how the upgrading process works. Let's say you've worked up to a regular clientele of 30 magazines and that's all you can carry.

The next step is begin to look for a market paying more than your present top market. When you find it, try it out for awhile and see if it's likely to become a regular—if it does, then drop your lowest-paying market.

As soon as your schedule stabilizes again, then start looking for another market that will pay more, and again when you've established it as a regular, drop the lower—this is just like climbing a ladder. If you watch for higher paying magazines and continually study what's being done, you'll find you can work up until some of your assignments are readily paying in the thousands.

Checking on Chapter 14

The first step in increasing your income is to build your reputation with a number of editors. Do this by working for as many magazines as possible in the beginning (not just once, however, but many, many times)—also, keep stressing the quality of your work—this includes photographs.

A success attitude is important. Know right from the beginning that you're going to make it.

Professional writers' organizations are useful. First they will acquaint you with successful writers in your field. They also will help in getting your name before editors.

Book credits make you more of an authority. This can be important when asking for assignments and also in setting rates.

Breaking into books is about like breaking into magazines. Query, then follow up positive replies with an outline, a table of contents, and two sample chapters.

After you are making a substantial income an agent can be of assistance. An agent can help increase your income through better marketing. He also can take the negotiating off your hands. Find agents by asking your publishers, other successful writers, and writing to the Society of Authors' Representatives for a list. Once you get an agent, you can't stop learning markets . . . . an agent can't do your job —he can only help.

Add columns and several-part series when possible. Practically every magazine is a candidate for a column or series article. Read the magazines and ask yourself, what do these readers need that's not now being offered?

Expenses help take the pressure off. You can often get expenses after you've done several articles for the same magazine by asking for them in your query.

Increased income means increased pressure. Systematically, go over possible markets and try to add ones that will pay more than you're now getting. Once you have all you can handle, drop your lowest-paying one.

CHAPTER 15

How to Resell Your Material Profitably

Making big money means wringing every last dollar out of your material. One of the biggest mistakes we writers make, of course, is to decide an article is dead once it has been sold.

With a little effort, you can sell some of your manuscripts over and over again to noncompeting fields. The whole secret is "noncompeting." This means you're selling your article to a magazine with an entirely different readership from the original market.

Some writers make a practice of wringing every possible sale out of each manuscript.

Rohn and Jeri Enghs, for instance, often sell the same article to as many as 15 publications under simultaneous submission.

All you do is simply put the words "simultaneous submission" on the upper right corner. The editor understands that this story is being offered to other publications in noncompeting fields. I tell my own students to put "exclusive, your field" which is, of course, the same thing. You can do this with many markets—newspapers, juvenile religious magazines, trade journals, and company publications. There are also others which you will find as you go along.

The all-time champ at this is Peter Simer, who at one time was a prisoner at Jackson, Michigan prison (and maybe he still is). He has been especially successful with submissions to company publications. One story, "Nobody Votes in My Town," sold 256 times for a total of $7471.70.

And now let's look at the fields more closely.

NEWSPAPERS ARE MULTIPLE-ARTICLE MARKETS

Newspapers circulate only in certain areas—Seattle newspapers, for example, are not read in Kansas City or Minneapolis. Therefore, the feature sections of these papers could certainly publish the same articles the same day.

A student of mine wrote a feature concerning a particular anniversary of the B-52 and sent copies to eight different newspapers in eight sections of the country where the crew members came from and received eight checks.

In syndicating articles to newspapers, first make sure their circulations do not overlap, then make separate copies and separate photographs for each.

Indicate in the right-hand corner that your article is being sent to other newspapers with "exclusive, your territory." Ordinarily, you also list the other newspapers it's being sent to also. A study of a number of newspapers will show you what kinds of features they're taking.

If possible, try to include a local tie-in for each market. Residency or former residency in the newspaper's circulation area of someone in the article is a good way to make it pertinent.

JUVENILE RELIGIOUS MAGAZINES
ALSO BUY SECOND RIGHTS

Actually they provide one of the best markets for reselling your material. Fortunately, the readers of the Baptist publications don't read Presbyterian publications, and Presbyterian readers don't read Methodist publications, and Methodists don't read the Catholic ones, and so forth. Therefore, very few editors will object to buying second rights. The terminology for this is "exclusive, your field" in the upper right-hand corner.

A student of mine did a story on a teen-age editor of a small-town newspaper, sent it out a number of times, and sold it to 11 religious magazines for a total of almost $600.

Again the rules are the same as they are for newspapers. Make an original of each article, make up separate pictures, mark it "simultaneous admission," and send it off. You must, of course, send for and study as many juvenile religious magazines as possible to determine exactly what they're taking.

IT'S POSSIBLE TO MIMEOGRAPH MANUSCRIPTS
FOR BUSINESS MARKETS

Mimeograph a manuscript? Never! I've learned long ago never say "Never" in the article-writing business. At one time or another, if you wait long enough, you'll be able to do everything. I find in the trade journal (business field), it's possible (if handled correctly) to sell mimeographed manuscripts.

Let me give you an example from my own experience. My first try at this was an article on reducing bad-debt losses by screening credit risk. Credit is a subject that plagues every retailer—since this article was about how to reduce credit losses, I realized it should be of interest to every business extending credit. I, therefore, went through *Standard Rate and Data Guide,* listing every field that used credit—this included drugstores, bicycle dealers, rental operators, feed and farm stores, photography shops, and more.

I then did a quite detailed article showing businessmen

exactly how to prescreen credit with indicators and guides. I also made up two pictures of credit applications, with big black arrows indicating the problem situations. When through, I picked out one magazine in each field and sent the mimeographed article with a note saying it was being offered "exclusive, your field." At that time I was unsure of how much to charge so I asked $35 an article. The results were 22 sold for $770.

Again, the thing to remember is that you need separate photographs for each. You also need to let the editor know you're submitting to other magazines outside his field. Do this by simply marking in the upper right-hand corner, "exclusive, your field."

COMPANY PUBLICATIONS ARE ADDITIONAL SALES MARKETS

Company magazines make good secondary markets. The reason is that these magazines seldom have overlapping circulations since they're usually sent to company customers or employees. Exceptions to this rule are the automobile manufacturer publications such as *Ford Times, Friends* (Chevrolet), and others with large audiences—these usually buy all rights and want first choice. Others, however, usually don't mind.

When you look, you'll find there are a lot of company publications that take general items, food, garden interests, outdoor sports, hobbies, travel, and others. If there's a good travel article in your files, for instance, get a copy of *Gebbie's House Magazine Directory* out of the library; go through and make a list of 15 or 20 publications that take general travel pieces and send it off, following the same rules we've outlined for other second-right submissions.

KEEP LOOKING FOR ADDITIONAL SECOND-RIGHT SALES SOURCES

Even after you've sold a particular article a number of times, don't give up—keep looking. Every time you pick up a magazine, see if you think it might be a possible second-right market for your article. If it looks good and the circulation doesn't overlap magazines you've sold before, by all means, send it off.

It's possible, of course, to do this systematically. All you have to do is use our old market-finding guide—that is, go to the table of contents of your *Writer's Market,* take each subject in turn, and ask yourself, "Would this group be interested in my article?" Let's say you have a piece on "party fortune-telling" that you've sold three or four times. Run through the index asking yourself, "Would automotive magazines be interested?" —answer yes or no. "Would photography magazines be interested?"—answer yes or no. "Would women's magazines be interested?"—answer yes or no. The answer here, of course, is "yes," some of them probably would. "Would the juveniles be interested?" Possibly, if you worked it right. And so on until you've covered all possible categories.

Then sit down and send off your manuscript to all possible markets. If you can, of course, you would improve sales chances considerably if you'd send for these magazines to make sure they're really a market for your article before submitting. Outside of articles for the four multiple-submission markets listed here, mark "second rights" in the upper right-hand corner of your manuscript.

TEN WAYS TO KEEP YOUR FILES ACTIVE AND ADD TO YOUR INCOME

Always keep looking for new and different ways to resell your material. Here are ten ways to do this:

1. Pull an article out of your files once a week and list all the possible markets. Don't initially think of particular magazines—think of interested groups.

Suppose, for instance, you have an article that sold to your local newspaper on the day-to-day workings of your local bank.

Now think of other possible markets. For instance, could

children be interested in how a bank works? Well, maybe not that particular bank—but children certainly could be interested in how a bank works in general. So think about the possibilities of changing the material around a bit, redoing a few of the sentences, and change the title to, for instance, "A Visit to a Bank" or "Here's How a Bank Works."

Also think in terms of other groupings. The same theme, or maybe the same article, for instance, with an insurance tie-in might interest the readers of insurance company magazines. You never know until you try.

2. Calendar every article to go out again in four years. When you finish getting all the mileage you can now from an article, don't write it off, but mark your calendar to "repull" it in four years. At this time, again go through all possible markets. Sometimes, with a few changes, you can send it back to the same magazine. Other times, that magazine has gone out of business and you can sell it to a competitor.

3. Take a particular magazine sometime and leaf through your files checking each article for a possible sale. Pick a house organ, for instance, say one that takes general travel articles. Look at two or three they've done, then go through your files asking if they'd be interested in this one, and so forth. You'd be surprised after you've built your files, how many additional sales you'll make this way.

4. Circulate a printed query (Figure 1). Here's a different one. Sometimes go through your files and pull four articles you think are especially good. Take the most illustrative photograph from each, make up to 2¼ inch size and paste up four to an 8 × 10 page, then have 50 copies printed at a quick printing service ($3 or $4 per 100). Send this out along with a note and let the editors check the ones they want. Some writers have done very well using this system.

5. Keep up with the new magazines. Any time you see an announcement of a new magazine or find a new one on the stands, go back through your files. Pull any article you think might possibly go and send it to them. New markets like this

Please Check the ones you want. Keep one copy of this query for your files.

HOUSEBOATING IS BOOMING AGAIN:
Although the houseboating fad slowed for awhile it is now coming on stronger than ever. This article details the many new developments and shows you the easy way to get in on the action.
1300 words.   Price $125.

THE NEW BOY SCOUTS:
The boy scouts today are undergoing radical changes. This article outlines what's happening and why:
1500 words.   Price $150.

EXPLORING THE DELTA
Northern California's San Joaquin-Sacramento Delta provides a fascinating vacation maze of waterways for fishermen, vacationists and family boaters. This article tells what to expect.
1800 words.   Price $200.

BICYCLING GOES BERSERK AGAIN.
After a one year lull the bicycle craze has taken off again like a skyrocket. While the last bicycle boom was based on an adult need for exercise, this one traces its origins directly to high gas prices. This article details what's happening now and predicts the possibilities for the future.
1500 words.   Price $180.

Figure 1

HOW TO RESELL YOUR MATERIAL PROFITABLY   245 often make excellent markets for second-right sales.

6. Be alert to new editors. New editors, like new magazines, often use a great deal of additional material right in the beginning. Many of them, like a new broom, sweep out the old editor's inventory and put in their own. This is a signal to go back through your files and see if you have anything that fits. I often do this in the trade journal field. If I have anything in a magazine's field that's topical and up-to-date, I'll pull it and send it in, offering second rights.

7. Make a list of reprint markets. Every time you find a magazine that will take second rights, put it on your list. When you do an article, then, instead of just sending it out once, mark down all possible markets. After the initial sale, run through your list until you've exhausted all possibilities.

8. Schedule a file review once a year. Take a week and do nothing but go through your files. Compare every article to your list of possible reprint markets. Don't try to second guess an editor. If you think he might be at all interested, by all means, pull the article and send it along. You'll be surprised how these pay off.

9. Have another writer look through your files occasionally. Some time have a friend go through and give you suggestions as to other places you can sell it. Often he'll look at it from a different point of view and can often suggest markets you've completely overlooked.

10. Pick an article you think is really good, then tell yourself you're not going to stop until you've made 50 or 100 sales (pick a figure).

Go through every possible channel, trying to market your article. Over the next year keep trying to push sales. Every time you pick up a magazine, ask yourself, "Is this a market?"

With special emphasis like this, you'll be surprised how many ways you'll find to sell this particular article. This may not seem very important but, by spotlighting it and concentrating attention, you'll sell it many more times than otherwise would be possible.

Checking on Chapter 15

Manuscripts can be sold many times. Reselling can be done in such fields as newspapers, juvenile religious markets, trade journals, company publications, and others. Manuscripts should be marked "simultaneous submission" or "second rights."

- *Newspapers buy simultaneous submissions, provided other sales are outside their circulation area. Study to determine what they're buying.*
- *Juvenile religious magazines of different denominations are second-rights markets. Publications take a wide variety of subjects.*
- *General business features can be sold to a number of business markets. They must take up some common businessman's problem like credit, shoplifting, accounting, bad checks, and similar subjects.*
- *Company magazines will buy features sold elsewhere first. General descriptions can be found in* Gebbie House Magazine Directory.
- *Many other publications buy articles published elsewhere first. If a magazine looks like a possible market, send them your manuscript plainly marked "second rights."*

Your files should be kept active. You can do this by: (1) pulling one article a week and listing all possible markets; (2) making sure articles sold several times get pulled again four years later; (3) taking one magazine and leafing through your files checking each article for a possible sale; (4) using printed-picture multiple queries; (5) checking new magazines regularly against your files; (6) making a mental check every time an editor changes to see if you have manuscripts that can be resold there; (7) making up your own reprint market list; (8) reviewing your files completely once a year for resale possibilities; (9) having another writer go over your material occasionally and make market suggestions; (10) concentrating on one particular article—set a sales goal and stay with it until accomplished.

Other Writer's Digest Books

Artist's Market, 409 pp. $10.95
Beginning Writer's Answer Book, 264 pp. $8.95
Cartoonist's and Gag Writer's Handbook, (paper), 157 pp. $8.95
Complete Guide to Marketing Magazine Articles, 248 pp. $8.95
Craft of Interviewing, 244 pp. $9.95
Craftworker's Market, 684 pp. $11.95
Creative Writer, 416 pp. $8.95
Guide to Writing History, 258 pp. $8.50
Handbook of Short Story Writing, 238 pp. $9.95
How to Be a Successful Housewife/Writer, 254 pp. $10.95
How to Write Short Stories that Sell, 228 pp. $9.95
How You Can Make $20,000 a Year Writing: No Matter Where You Live, 270 pp. (cloth) $10.95; (paper) $6.95
Law and the Writer, 240 pp. $9.95
Magazine Writing: The Inside Angle, 256 pp. $10.95
Magazine Writing Today, 220 pp. $9.95
Mystery Writer's Handbook, 273 pp. $8.95
1001 Article Ideas, 270 pp. $10.95
One Way to Write Your Novel, 138 pp. $8.95
Photographer's Market, 613 pp. $12.95
The Poet and the Poem, 399 pp. $11.95
Sell Copy, 205 pp. $11.95
Songwriter's Market, 426 pp. $10.95
Stalking the Feature Story, 310 pp. $9.95
Successful Outdoor Writing, 244 pp. $11.95
Travel Writer's Handbook, 288 pp. $11.95
Treasury of Tips for Writers, 174 pp. $7.95
Writer's Market, 901 pp. $14.95
Writer's Resource Guide, 488 pp. $12.95
Writing and Selling Non-Fiction, 317 pp. $10.95
Writing and Selling Science Fiction, 191 pp. $8.95
Writing for Children & Teenagers, 269 pp. $9.95
Writing for Regional Publications, 203 pp. $11.95
Writing the Novel: From Plot to Print, 197 pp. $10.95
Writing Popular Fiction, 232 pp. $8.95

To order directly from the publisher, include $1.25 postage and handling for 1-2 books; for 3 or more books, include an additional 25¢ for each book. Allow 30 days for delivery.

For a current catalog of books for writers, write to Department B, **Writer's Digest Books, 9933 Alliance Road, Cincinnati OH 45242**

Prices subject to change without notice.